Harry Wayne Adda

MAMA Was a Con Man,
PAPA Was a Christian

Also by Harry Wayne Addison

Write That Down for Me, Daddy
RFD #3

MAMA Was a Con Man, PAPA Was a Christian

HARRY WAYNE ADDISON

PELICAN PUBLISHING COMPANY

Gretna 1992

First printing, 1989
Second printing, 1992

Library of Congress Cataloging-in-Publication Data

Addison, Harry Wayne.
    Mama was a con man, papa was a Christian / by Harry Wayne
Addison.
        p. cm.
    ISBN 0-88289-714-4
    1. Country life—Louisiana—Fiction. 2. Depressions—1929—
Fiction. 3. Louisiana—Fiction. I. Title.
PS3551.D398M3 1989
813′.54—dc19   88-27586
                                                             CIP

Manufactured in the United States of America

Published by Pelican Publishing Company, Inc.
1101 Monroe Street, Gretna, Louisiana 70053

*To Lil, my wife, who deciphered my hastily
scribbled recollections of yesteryear, and
did it patiently at an indifferent typewriter. . . .*

CONTENTS

MAMA Was a Con Man, PAPA Was a Christian

MAMA AND PAPA

I know Mama was a con man, 'cause back during the depression, she had all of us kids thinking tripe was deep-sea fish. And I never doubted Papa was a "born-again Christian," 'cause I've heard him say blessin's over leftover tripe, and it took a man of God to say it the first time!

We'd been "pants-patching poor" for a long time, and then the depression came along and things got worse. The gypsies came through and took their mark off our gate and Mama even let me, Ed, Carl, and Betty Gene play with their kids, but they sent us home, saying "we was so ragged we'd give 'em a bad name."

It was hot that summer in Swartz in North Louisiana and I remember Old John Swinney had hollered at us from the road, 'n I could tell by the way he was walkin' that he'd been doin' some more backslidin' and they had to start prayer circle for 'im all over again. Seemed just yesterday he'd come down the aisle at the Lock Arbor Baptist Church. We'd jus' got through singin' the last verse of "Why Not Tonight?" for the fourth time even if it was the midday service, when we heard 'im groan and then start bawlin' and comin' down front, wantin' to repent and git his sins washed away. The preacher was tugging at the pulpit and the song leader was hepin' 'im shove, 'cause they didn't waste no time gitting a man "emersed" and of course the baptismal was under the floor beneath the pulpit.

Well, sir, by the time all the deacons got through layin' hands on Old John, the preacher led him down the steps 'n into the water 'n didn't even take no time to warm it up. The preacher laid him back and kinda sloshed him 'round 'cause he wanted to make sure he kept him under long enough. Old John came up sputterin' and fightin' and cold and blue as a possum. But, he was back for Bible Training Union 'n night preachin', wearin' a tie and clean white socks.

Come Monday morning, Old John was drunker 'n Cooter Brown 'n fightin' 'n "pie rootin'" every day of the week. But on Sunday, down the aisle he came, cryin', confessin', and wantin' to be forgiven and have his sins rinsed away again. The preacher saw 'im coming and had the vat open by the time he reached the last pew. That Sunday, he held him under uncommonly long,

11

and that evening Old John wanted a part on the BTU program and got it. 'Course, Baptists will bridle you up and have you plowin' 'fore you're used to the hames. The next week came with Old John drinkin' 'n sinnin' as usual, but Sunday morn, he'd be bawling down to the front onct more. It happened with such frequency that the Board of Deacons gave the pastor permission just to meet Old John out front before services and hose him down. Old John kept on sinnin' but his evil ways dropped off appreciably during the cold snaps. Come summer days, though, and the hosing and hollering would pick up all over again. He was singing "Why Not Tonight?" as he disappeared down the dusty road.

Mama had come out on the porch and was watching us watch Old John and admonished us with "If you boys don't quit that lollygagging and get to work, I'm gonna skin you alive." I never could picture Mama standing up there on that porch holding one of our hides and saying, "I told you so," but that threat would move a mule and we took to the chores.

Then on Sunday, right after preaching, 'bout 1:30, they said that if everything went right, there was to be a funeral for old Zeb from down in the Colony. Oh, he'd lived a long time, and he a'ready said he was spent and tried to die four or five times a'fore, but never could find a spot that was convenient to turn loose.

I'd never been to any buryin's outside of RFD #3, 'cept at Mansfield, and it was such a remarkable difference in the number of pallbearers that I was bustin' to count 'em at Springhill Cemetery. Sure enough, when the big, old black hearse came to a stop and the dust settled, the head paller came 'round in back lookin' like he'd rehearsed his part. The next four stood holding a fifty-pound paper bag by each corner, facing the head paller. Then the other six stood ready for the box to be unloaded. The rope men stood by to lower the body in the hole and, at a signal, the ten men headed to the grave site, led by the head paller and preacher.

When they reached the grave, the preacher stepped to one side, the lead man walked around the opening opposite the mourners, and the four men straddled the grave with the sack. As soon as they got set, the head paller pulled a barlow knife from his pocket and reached under and split the bag from end to end. The four then shook the contents into the freshly dug grave. Then at a signal, they dropped the empty container into the hole. Then they stepped aside for the six men to position the box on the poles set across for supports until the readin' and prayin' was done. Everybody stood 'round with an uncomfortable-like look and feeling, such as, "I ain't gonna die for a long while; maybe I ain't gonna never die," but knowing us all would.

After the close kin left, the rope men came up and lowered the box ever so gently, then shoveled in the old white clay mud until it became a mound. I'd been holding Papa's hand so as not to be "swooped" away by the death angels, and finally looked up to ask why we allus had eleven pallbearers when Mansfield had only six. Papa barely whispered it was "'cause this old dirt at Swartz's so poor you have to fertilize the grave for the soul to rise." I never asked no more.

I woke up Wednesday morning still thinking about old Zeb in that box, but he probably wadn't thinkin' 'bout us folks he'd left behind, 'cause the preacher said, "Those that crossed to the other side wadn't thinkin' 'bout nothin' sad" and he sure wadn't thinkin' 'bout a depression and fried tripe.

Mama called and I answered sleepily, "Yes'm."

"Milk time, boy."

"Yes'm, durn ole cows."

"What you say, boy?"

"Nothin', Mama." I didn't want Mama stirred up. I still remembered the time Papa had flogged me 'bout somethin' I said.

I can still remember my bottom burning. Seemed no longer'n a week past that I'd copied the license number off the old Model T Ford we usta own and had run it up to Mama Morrow. I wanted her to crank up their old Durrant auto and take me to Monroe so's I could turn Papa's name in to Sheriff Coverdale, and I thought he needed the license number to identify Papa. Well, Mama Morrow thought that was the funniest thing she ever had heard and told Papa. He didn't see no humor in it at all. He proceeded to give me an unbroken dose of a "tearing up my backside," and when he turned me loose, I was sporting the reddest rear on the RFD. Now, Papa was pretty deaf, and as I walked out past the washpot and he walked out the front gate a good piece from where I was rubbing my rump, I softly muttered between sobs that "I wished that one-pound Morning Joy coffee can was full of lead; I'd throw it at 'im." Well, sir, he heard me somehow, and when he turned me loose the third time, my britches wouldn't a held shucks.

After that, I wouldn't a hid behind Canterberry's split-log barn with the wind blowin' in my face and the thunder rollin', lightning flashing, and cows bellerin' 'n whisper nothin' 'bout Papa 'cept things you could say in front of God.

When I got through milking that morning, Mama had me some breakfast ready: biscuits, grits, home-cured ham, two yard eggs, and a glass of sweet milk to wash it all down. I loved grits with lots of homemade butter, anyhow.

Mama was a good cook, too, but she'd make a big "to do" about packing our lunches for school. At the beginning of every school year, she would call allus kids together and go through the "sack ceremony." "Here's yours, Harry Boy, and you daren't lose it or you'll have to carry your lunch in your pockets again and you never did like lint on your biscuits!" Boy, we'd hold onto them sacks 'til they got so greasy an ant couldn't a climbed 'em, even if they'd take a running start. We'd allus fold 'em and bring 'em home in back of our geography books, 'til you could get a snack by gnawing on the back cover.

Well, those city kids had them side-opening lunch buckets and I wanted one so bad, I just pained. 'Sides, they'd open 'em with a flair. If you didn't watch 'em, they'd clear their throat so's you'd look, and 'fore you looked off, they'd "flair you." There ain't no way you can open a sack with a flair. You just got down in 'em and got ya'self somethin' lookin' half-dead. Another thing they had was little old bitty light bread sandwiches, wrapped in waxed paper with the crust trimmed off, and it was a dead giveaway that we were "country," because you can't trim a biscuit.

Mama asked me what I was daydreaming about, and when I said, "Side openers," she replied, "Boy, you do beat all I have ever seen. Now, finish your breakfast and go down to the Red Store for me. Take this list and don't hang around, 'n get back home."

"Yes'm," I replied.

I got back just after the noon whistle blew and I knew Mama was gonna be walkin' and talkin' and I wadn't wrong!

"But Mama, you oughta been 'nair. Old Joe Ragan was in 'is wagon and had been to Monroe. He had his cows, calves, goats, guineas, geese, hogs, plows, dressers, bedsteads, and all piled up higher'n his head. Said he'd 'got one of them last letters' from

14

the bank, that they's comin' after everythin' he had, so he jus' took it to 'em. He said he drove right up on the sidewalk by the bank and took a hoe handle and whacked the side wall and hollered, 'Y'all come on out 'cheer, y'all heah me?' Whack! 'Come on out 'cheer, right now.' Whack! Ragan said everybody in the bank came runnin' out to see what was causin' all the ruckus, and when one of the ladies saw what all he had on 'at wagon and tied to it, she jus' up and fainted. Said you coulda heard 'em guineas 'per rackin'' plumb out to Sicard."

The bank president had come trotting out to see what all the commotion was and old Joe Ragan bellowed out at 'im. "Heah it is, all of it. You wanted it and now heah it is!"

Old Joe said he jumped off the wagon and headed home, the bank president right behind 'im. Old Joe never slowed a whit. Said he jus' commenced to walking faster. By then the president was beggin', "Now, come on, Mr. Ragan. You need to take your stock and wagon home."

Old Joe said, "I kinda slowed down and said, a'right, I'm gonna take this old stuff back, but I need some time and I don't want no more botherin' duns."

"Yes, Mr. Ragan, we won't send you any more duns, just please come get these cows off the sidewalk and don't worry about all that mess. Our janitor can clean off all of this. Here, let me help you up in the wagon. Have a good trip home."

Old Joe Ragan was built like a barrel, and his belly was jumping up and down as he told how nice they treated him, laughin' to beat "ole Dan" after the doctor.

"Well, Mama, I jus' couldn't leave 'til Mr. Joe finished. You oughta seen his wagon, Mama! You jus' oughta seen it!"

"Where's the flour, boy?"

"Lordy mercy, Mama, I bet you I forgot it down at the store. I'll be right back, Mama."

I could still see old Joe's wagon and I knew I was in for it, 'cause he'd done got 'im a fresh bunch listening and his story had probably got better 'n I'd have to listen to the new one. Papa'd be home by the time I was, but he'd been a boy onct and he'd be easier to reckon with. 'Sides, though, Mama knew, too. . . .

We ate corn bread that night but we had a new unopened sack of flour, caused by a delayed delivery.

15

Next morning, we was gonna have us the best rally you ever saw, if it didn't rain. Tin can shinny or "whip your buddy" marbles, and it was gonna be "keeps." Preacher said we ought'n to play for keeps 'cause it was gamblin', but heck, it wadn't no fun without takin' a chanct. We played mumbly peg, too, but old Burton'd beat us ever' time. You just couldn't drive a peg in the ground deep enough to keep 'im from pullin' it out with his teeth. 'Cept he'd played so much, the grit done wore his teeth off up front to the gums. 'Course his gums was so tough he could pull a lightered stump outa the new ground with a sore mouth.

"Boy," Papa called.

"Yes, sir."

"You know what time it is?"

"No, sir."

"It's dark. You go milk those cows and slop the hogs."

"Yes, sir. Old Abe Lincoln ain't never heard of me."

"What'd you say, boy?"

"Nothin', jus' thinkin' 'bout the Civil War, Papa."

"That's fine. It's good to learn about your country."

Papa was somethin'! He'd only been to the third grade but he knew more stuff 'bout everything 'n could work a crossword puzzle without cheatin' or 'rasin' out nothin'. He never got to go to school much. He just learned 'cause he wanted to or had to. Wish I could get that feelin' 'fore next year.

I had to walk careful 'cause the night was dark with cloud cover and the moon was mostly blind.

Tomorrow, it'd be raining, so I might as well forget about having our rally. But right now I better be at milking and slopping so's I could get to bed.

Mama was allus scared of clouds 'n lightning 'n wind, 'n come to think of it, she was scared of lots of things, 'less you messed with her young'ns. Then she'd bow up like a cutworm, like she did when Old Man Chapmon called Carl "four eyes" 'cause he had to wear specs. Boy, she was ten feet high that morning and still growing.

I let the calf in while I went to slop the hogs. They didn't care whether they could see or not, long as they got fed. When I got back and took the calf away from its mama, I rinsed her off again, took the cream, turned the cows out, and gave the calves some cottonseed meal and hulls.

I went to bed praying for sunshine for tomorrow and next thing I heard was a booming clap of thunder, waking everything in the country and stirring some of the folks in Springhill Cemetery.

Mama had coffee made and said it was 5:30 and the cows were bellowing to be milked. The rain was coming down so hard, I could just barely see the cow shed.

I took a croaker sack to the cows and rubbed 'em down so's not to get water dripped in the pail, and set to milking.

The lightning was something to see, splittin' the ears and runnin' its forked tongue ever' which way. I heard Old John sloshin' down the road singing "Why Not Tonight?" at the top of his voice, and pausing just long enough to take a long drag of his bottle. All of a sudden, the road lit up like it was on fire and it seemed like a bolt of flame done hit Old John. Well, sir, I heard old Swinney holler, "Oh, Lord God A'mighty, don't hit me no more." Nex', I knew he was in the middle of the road on his knees prayin' . . . his whiskey bottle had a strange glow in the ditch, still afire. And he didn't have no shoes on and he was as white as the milk in the bucket.

Old John Swinney done found the Lord sure as sin and he was some kinda preacher after that night.

He'd fought so many fights, his nose was crooked as a dog's hind leg, 'n you couldn't a found a sin he hadn't looked straight in the eye. So, you couldn't lie outa your evil ways with John. Matter a fact, one time outside the Red Store, I myself heard him tell one of the Larcy brothers, if he didn't come down the aisle next Sunday, he'd forgive him 'cause he was a Christian but 'cause he was human he was gonna whup his backside 'til he found God.

Another thing John did, he made his favorite hymn the national anthem of RFD #3.

And even now, decades later, the hair on my nape still stands at attention and I'm tempted to walk down the aisle agin whenever I hear "Why Not Tonight?"

To comprehend the immeasurability of space is to be able to fathom the omnipotence of God.

17

DOC'S DOSE

The old man felt dizzy, wiped his brow with the back of his hand, and leaned against his workbench. The spell soon passed and he picked up his hammer and began to tap lightly at the rusted bolt to loosen it. After a few taps, he tried his wrench again, to no avail. He reached high on a shelf to get a length of pipe that he used on his wrench as a cheater, so it would give him more leverage. In stretching, he felt a sharp pain deep in his chest and stopped short. He rested a moment and took a deep breath. The hurt was there again, but this time he racked with a deep rattling cough that left him faint. He put his tools back in place and walked slowly to the house. His wife watched him as he came closer and she moved out on the porch to ask him if he felt alright. He did not answer until he reached the top of the stairs. He caught on to the cane-bottom chair, and by then his breath was a short gasp.

"Go get ole Doc, would ya?"

"Well, let me get you in bed, Amos; you need to be in bed." She busied herself in making him comfortable, then stripping off her apron, started toward their neighbor's house. She was almost running when she got halfway there and Mrs. Hunt had noticed with concern her hurried approach.

"Mrs. Hunt, Mrs. Hunt, where's your husband?" she called.

Mrs. Hunt turned on her heels and disappeared back into the house, and by the time Mrs. Warden had reached the front gate, Mr. and Mrs. Hunt were coming through the front door.

"It's Amos—he may be having a heart attack or something!" Mrs. Warden gasped.

Mr. Hunt said, "You go on home and I'll go get Doc. Now don't you worry none."

Mrs. Warden turned and started back to Amos.

Mr. Hunt walked straight to the garage, hoping the old car would start.

After a few chokes and patting the accelerator, the engine sputtered, coughed, and began hitting on three cylinders, then four, then three, then evened off on four as he eased the car out of the garage and headed for old Doc's house.

Doc didn't have an office; he just worked out of his home. Mr. Hunt drove up in Doc's yard, horn blaring.

Old Doc came to the door, bleary-eyed, and hollered, "What the hell's going on?"

Mr. Hunt jumped out of his car and ran up on the porch. He could tell before he got close that old Doc was on one. When he decided to go on a drunk, you just made ready, because he hung on a ringed-tail tooter.

"It's Amos Warden, Doc—he's sick and needs you," Mr. Hunt said apologetically, for having had to interrupt the drinking spree.

"Well, let me get my gear," Doc muttered, going back inside, opening his black bag, and placing some standard "cure-alls" and a quart of good whiskey inside. He looked for a couple more but they had been found earlier.

The pair drove up in Amos's yard and walked on in the house without knocking, for they knew they were expected. Doc took one look at Amos and told the rest to clear the room.

Mrs. Warden asked, "Me, too?"

"Hell yes, everybody means everybody but me and Amos."

Mrs. Warden and all the neighbors who had come over departed.

Muffled voices could be heard from the room but no one could discern what was being said. After a spell, Doc stepped to the door and said simply, "Amos has pneumonia. Now, I want me a couple o' more quarts of this whiskey and I want it now." With that he closed the door.

Mrs. Hunt went straight to the whiskey store and returned with Doc's prescription. She tapped lightly at the door and the only thing that anyone saw was Doc's hand reaching out for his order. When Doc closed the door, nobody was going in or out until he opened it again. No one ever knew what Doc did behind those closed doors, but he just never let any corpse come out. One man who was waiting with Mrs. Warden said he remembered just a little about what happened when Doc pulled him through. He claimed old Doc had poured two glasses of whiskey and said, "You drink yours and I'll drink mine. It may not cure you, but you won't give a damn what you got."

Someone spoke up and asked, "Is that all you remember?"

"Well, I lived and 'at's more'n most folks who get it can say," he answered.

19

The man next to him was sipping on a saucer of coffee and noticed Mrs. Warden was crying. He stood up and said, "Mrs. Warden, don't you worry none 'bout ole Amos. Doc might have whiskey on his breath but he's got whupping death on his mind."

The days dragged on and people hovered around the door. The only noise coming from the sickroom was Doc's voice "cussing" the devil for being a thief of souls and stating he was damned if he was turning loose of old Amos.

Finally, the door opened and old Doc appeared, with a growth of beard, red eyes, and a rumpled suit. Why, just the sight of him would scare the hell out of the devil!

"Get Amos some soup and clean long handles. If he don't make it now, I've wasted some good booze."

The parson bowed his head and whispered, "Dear God, thank you for all your mercies, good medication, and this old drunk. Amen."

Amos was calling his wife.

Everyone I have ever known has had moments of genius. The ones who have become successful or famous are they who did not let those moments die, but persevered on and on and on, multiplying those moments into hours, hours into days, days into years until their goals were finally achieved.

THE KILLING

Two big, fat hogs had been scalded, scraped, and were hanging ready to be gutted on the oak tree limb. The weather had blown cold enough to keep pork from spoiling until it was rubbed with Morton's salt and hung in the smokehouse for curing. I loved the smell of the hickory smoldering as it clung to your clothes and hung in the air on a frosty morning when meat was needed. It was almost a compliment to go fetch a slab of side meat for Mama's kitchen.

Papa had filed his knives razor sharp and was trimming the lean strips from the fat, and if I live to be a hundred, I will always remember the smell of fresh pork strips and biscuits cooking. Just add a lot of homemade butter and syrup and all the stench of wet hog bristles would disappear from my memory.

Over the years, I have often thought of how simple life was only a little while ago. The 1920s were wild to a few, and they made the news, but for most Americans, it was a time of great tranquility and progress. People were listening to more radios, riding in better cars, and burning natural gas in their ranges. It was cheap gas that would last forever. Even in the yard around the washpot, the fire burned night and day.

The winter moved in and so did folks who didn't have chores to keep them out of doors. Mama and Papa were sitting by the fire talking about a man who had died down the road. Someone had gotten drunk and stabbed him. The sheriff had picked up a man who had been in and out of jail more than the sweeper and he'd probably be out and drunk again before tomorrow evening.

I asked Papa who the man was and he looked over his glasses and said, "Old man, it's time you were in bed. Now scoot."

Mama lowered her voice when they began talking again. I couldn't make out a thing Papa was saying, either. I strained to hear what they were saying, and the next thing I knew, it was morning.

The funeral for the stabbed man was a long, drawn-out country service where the preacher warned everyone about how uncertain life was and they ought to be ready. He knew his Bible, but he couldn't remember the man's name and it angered me that the corpse was used as a threat.

21

Papa sensed my disgust and quieted me with a look. I whispered to Papa about the way the parson acted and what he said and I couldn't understand why a dead man should be showed off that way.

Papa looked at me a long time and asked in a hushed tone, "Old man, when you go out to gather tomatoes, don't you get all the ripe ones?"

"Yes, sir," I replied.

"Well, son, that's all the preacher's trying to do." With that, he sat silent and so did I.

The cold wind blew the wreath over on the grave. The pallbearers were shaking hands with the widow. Her children, too young to know what had happened, wandered away.

The coffin was the same color as the barrel we had scalded the hogs in.

Man and beast felled by the knife.

No one would ever miss the hog.

I wish I could remember the man's name. . . .

AS THE TWIGS

Papa had drained the radiator of the old Model T Ford, because the weather had turned much colder since milking time, and one thing that's hard to wake up to is a "busted block" in a car.

The stock would sleep in the sheds tonight, if they were lucky. And if Ma Perkins "cussed" this evening, it would be spring before her words would thaw.

Persimmons and collards would sweeten to where anybody would eat them.

I had on my long handles and thick cotton socks to keep from aching in the night, for cold, like poverty, is hard to get comfortable in.

Mama had every cover in the house out of the "quilt box," and still clucked around her nest scratching up more warmth.

The folks had been worried about my health, because I would always wake up as tired as I was when I went to bed. It only happened in the winter months and that was unusual, for only cold germs liked cold weather.

I hit the bed shivering and about midnight I awoke to an ache in my shoulders. I got up, wrapped a quilt around me, and went in to sit by the fire. I dropped off to sleep, and later realized why I was seemingly anemic. I had just been worn out from toting covers every night to keep from freezing.

I was lucky, but my brother was marked for life. He always slept on his back and the weight of the quilt bent his legs outward like twigs. Even now, many years later, he is still slew-footed.

Thus we spent our formative years.

My longest day was when I tried to be someone other than me. . . .

LEARNING HOW TO LIE

Mama was a great cook, good mother, haphazard housekeeper, and charming, chaotic citizen. She had learned an old Indian trick, I suppose, from the "Rap a Ho's." I never saw her do it, because it scared me so bad I'd always close my eyes and miss it. It was called "skinning you alive." She would always conclude any big warning with "you boys do that one more time, and I'm going to skin you alive."

"Yes, mam, Mama," was our stock answer. Because by this time, Carl and I had become proficient prevaricators.

One day, I remember Mama was standing on the porch. She was a short woman. She could walk under Papa's outstretched arm, but up there on that porch she looked twelve feet tall, and on her right hand she had a three-foot finger that directed us.

Mama admonished us to stay away from that dirty swimming hole. "Don't you dare go in that mud pond or I'll skin you alive!"

"No mam, we won't, Mama," we replied.

Later on in the day we came dragging home, as filthy as we could get, and Mama was on the veranda, waiting with that yardstick finger.

"Come here, boys," she commanded as she reached for Carl's hair. If it was still wet, it would be her barometer, and she could split hairs on the moisture content.

"You been in that creek, boy?"

"No, mam, Mama."

"What's your hair doing damp, then?"

"Harry pumped water on my head down at the Perkins' pump," he declared.

"Is that right, Harry Boy?" Mama quickly asked.

"Yes, mam, Mama." I corroborated the lie. "I pumped water on him down at the Perkins' pump."

"Did you go in that stinking creek, Harry?"

"No, mam, Mama."

"Well, what were you doing while Carl and the others were swimming?" Mama queried.

"I'ze sitting on the bank watchin' 'em, Mama."

Mama got out her skinning knife and when she finished him, old Carl took me behind the feed house and thumped me.

We both kept up the learning of lying and becoming better swimmers, and Mama will someday be compared to Bowie and his knife.

But her fame will be her skinning with a switch.

Good news travels as fast as bad news—it just doesn't make as much noise.

SOMETHING "EXTRA"

The old doctor was as dedicated to his profession as a man could be. He thanked the good Lord many times that his parents were well-to-do, for once again he had taken a couple of more geese in as payment on a long-overdue bill. Sometimes, his buggy would have crates tied all over it. Once, he even had a goat tied on behind. Nobody told him this was the way the practice of medicine paid off. And it was some dose! He climbed out of his surrey and called to Cain, his black manservant.

"Yas, suh, well, suh I sees you got us some mo' geese. We gots geese evahwhere and evah coop we has is full of 'em honkin', messy mouths."

"Cain, just get the geese," the doctor directed.

"Yas, suh."

The doctor opened his mail and read anew about the new-fangled thing called a horseless carriage. He took his pipe out of his mouth and sipped on some wine that Cain had brought him.

"Man, that's good," he observed. Then he spoke to his wife. "Abby, you know, I think I'm going to buy me one of those new contraptions. That is, if they'll take geese in on a trade!"

"What new contraption are you talking about now?" she asked.

The doctor handed her the pamphlet.

"They'll never last. You better keep your horse," was her judgment.

"Aw, I'm not going to learn how to drive the fool thing," he said. "I'm going to have them teach Cain."

So Cain was trained to drive the "fool thing" and the doctor was his faithful fare. They never got anyplace on time in the car because of the constant admonitions of the backseat driver, who didn't know the radiator from the rear end. Cain drove with great aplomb, in any case.

The roads, if you could call them that, were awful, even in the best of weather, and it jostled the doctor's being to where he swore he was going to go get his geese back.

Early one morn, the pair climbed into their respective places and were barked at, on the way, by all the neighborhood dogs. The doctor was busily giving instructions where they would go first and Cain knew they were in for it. The roads in that area were hog wallows or worse.

The doctor was a great admirer of well-bred cows and as they neared a meadow on the way home, after a day of rounds with the usual barter of chickens, guineas, ducks, and other sundry small clucking, peeping things tied here and there, he noticed a herd of cattle. Cain pulled back on the steering wheel as though he were still driving the surrey. But he did remember to apply the brakes properly and slid to a stop. The doctor stepped out in the mud and made his way over to the fence for a closer look at the cows. While the doctor was making his inspection, Cain got out and noticed a bulbous projection between the rim and casing on the left rear wheel. He had never seen an inner tube, especially one that had wormed its way out of its encasement.

Cain called to the doctor and described the "symptoms," whereupon the doctor turned, rubbed his chin, and diagnosed in a medical way by saying, "Hell, Cain, if you're not sure, operate."

"Say what?" questioned Cain.

"Take your knife and cut the fool thing off," the doctor replied and turned back to his cattle gazing.

Shortly thereafter, a loud "kapow" was heard, and as the medical man turned, he observed the backside of his driver clearing a fence and rapidly moving on. The doctor moved to the site of the operation and was greeted with the sight of his first flat tire.

Cain was coaxed patiently back to the wheel, and as they limped home on a rim, the doctor muttered, "Someday, Cain, somebody will have enough sense to put an extra on these fool contraptions."

Thus he put into motion an item of standard equipment in motoring across America.

Cain answered a question on his own future by saying, "I ain't goin' nevah operate on no more of yoah patients."

And with that decision, Ouachita Parish may have lost its first black surgeon.

If you've ever had to sit in a doctor's office, you know why he refers to his clients as "patients."

DAMNING EVIDENCE

My schoolteacher was from Monroe and she was a really nice lady—friendly but stern. Most of all, though, she was generous. One morning, she came to school with a small puppy, a fuzzy ball of fur. I was chosen as its new master. I named her "Tot" for that's what everyone called my teach.

Tot was never a large dog, except for her heart. She was devoted to me and I to her. We roamed the woods and byways together as two hunters, examining every hole and hollow tree, ferreting out imaginary game, chasing rabbits, and flushing birds, especially the chickens at home. She was a Spitz, and she was a good mama. She bore many offsprings that I gave away. When she got up in years, I decided I would keep one of her sons to be my companion when she chose to lie by the fire and dream of the days we had foraged while young.

Tot bore two short-haired pups, one black with white markings and one white with black spots. My oldest brother, Ed, wanted the black one and I, of course, took the other. We named them Hans and Fritz after the comic strip kids.

Fritz was to live only a few weeks, because a car wheel snuffed out his life, but Hans grew into a muscular sleek animal and he was mine. Hans was born with a short tail, and about an inch from the end, it was bent back as though nature had de-tailed him. It looked like a thumb crooked at the end. The neighbor's son could never say Hans and forthwith called him Damn Dog, which was forever to be his name. You could hear him being called all through the Quarters: "Here, Damn Dog! Here, Damn Dog!" So, Damn Dog and I took over the trails that Tot and I had trod, and discovered new places and things neither of us had ever dreamed of.

Damn Dog was to live for several years and so was Tot, who in time had become gray and was forced to eat soft food because of the loss of teeth.

One day, Damn Dog disappeared and it would be years before I learned a neighbor had killed him. I grieved for him for a long time and only Tot kept me from complete despair. . . . Then Tot died.

I now believe that God gives children pets who die or are killed while young to acclimate us to the reality that all things come to an end, no matter how much we love them. We are thus trained to overcome our sadness and shape up so that we may face tomorrow.

But, we still cry. . . .

God did not give me what I asked for, He gave me what I needed—thank God He did not give me what I deserved.

FLOODED OUT

The floorboard of the old Model T had little pools of water that nagged at the long-collected dust, turning it slowly into tiny riverlets of mud. Papa eased the car through the floodwaters while us kids watched animals and snakes lose their timidity as they sought higher ground. Papa was telling Mama about some of the men who had recently returned from Vicksburg, Mississippi. "Said they'd run a motorboat right straight down the Dixie Overland Highway without touching nothing." One crew had lost a motor and their boat because they'd run over a barbed wire fence and the propellor had wound the wire up 'til it pulled the boat under.

Papa glanced back over his shoulder and told us to keep our feet up on the seats so they'd be dry. Boy, I thought, that was something! He'd usually thump us for having our brogans on the cushions.

Papa drove slowly around the curve at Joe White's road, where the water was coming over the banks of Bayou DeSiard, and pulled the spark and gas levers down a little to pick up some speed. We must have been doing nineteen miles per hour when he braked down for Sicard Curve. Well, everybody knew it wasn't called "Dead Man's Curve" for nothing. Why, I myself had seen three or four T's lying on their backsides, wheels spinning, like run-over creatures kicking up their heels.

The water had run out of the insides of the old car and Papa said he thought it would be alright to put our feet down now. He didn't have to check on us, because he was easy to understand when he told you what or what not to do. All in all, he was the best Papa I'd ever seen—strict, but with a streak of kindness bigger than he was.

By and by, he pulled the T over in front of Baer's store on DeSiard Street in Monroe, and we all piled out. The first thing we heard was some folks talking about the guards patrolling the levee. They said they'd had orders to shoot trespassers, because if the levee broke or somebody dynamited it, all of Monroe would go under.

Papa stopped us in a wad and gave us our orders. "Now, boys, this is very serious and I want you to stay nearby, and after

Mama and your sister do their shopping, I'll take you down to the levee and let you have a look."

We stood as close to the pool hall as country Christians could so that we could hear the "grown-ups" inside talking about the high waters.

"Why, I betcha I seen a hundred cows floating down through Richland Parish," one bewhiskered old man offered.

"That ain't nothin'" spoke up another. "Why, I seen four houses with whole families, goats, chickens, and dogs float plumb acrost the road in front of my very own eyes!"

The stories grew longer and stronger as the bubbly brew filled the thirsty storytellers.

As soon as Mama got through talking to Mama Baer and catching up on all the city folks' activities, we gawked down DeSiard Street, beyond the Palace and up by the Louisiana Hotel, where some young women were leaning out the windows hollering something. South Grand was packed with sandbags and the water was bleeding through. As we neared the railroad crossing, we could see the levee well, the uniformed soldiers with their rifles walking back and forth along the sandbags. Papa lifted Betty Gene up on his shoulders so she could get a closer look. We heard her squeal with delight as she told us a tree was floating by.

I climbed a pole so I could get a better view, and wondered at the water swirling in little liquid tornados as it sped past Monroe.

Papa said, "We ought to head for home before dark, and besides, the chores are waiting." One thing in our favor was that Swartz was on a ridge and the floodwaters didn't come any higher than the tree line, so we would be safe and dry. Besides, you didn't have to drive up the cows because they stayed close to home.

We loaded in the flivver, Papa cranked her up, and we clattered out of town. The conversation was about nothing but the terrible loss of property and cattle, and human miseries. It seemed such an overwhelming calamity . . . yet we were survivors.

Papa was motoring about as fast as he could when he interrupted Mama's thought with "That's Old John's car up there by Ingleside, ain't it?"

"Yes, it is," Mama answered.

31

We slowed down to see what he was troubled with and found him fuming and kicking at the wheels and swearing something fierce.

"What's a matter, John?" Papa asked.

"This dad-blamed pile of junk ain't worth two whoops in Hades," muttered the cantankerous old man. John lived on one of the highest ridges in the area, so he was completely above the threat of the inundation.

Papa got out of the car, went around John's car, and lifted the hood. He fiddled around with the carburetor for a while and told John to get behind the wheel and let him crank it a spin or two. Old John was still hot under the collar and muttering about "what hard luck God allus sent him." Papa lifted up on the crank, gave it a few quick turns, and the old car sputtered to life.

John was in no mood to thank anybody. He just drove off cussing!

Papa crawled back in our T, shaking his head.

Mama asked, "What was wrong with his car?"

"Aw, he was just having a taste of what most folks are getting a bait of . . . just flooded out."

I heard Betty Gene say "I ummm, I bet God's gonna get him for all that cussin'."

I was seven years old during that flood of '27.

Take time for others, and if you take the I and ME out of TIME, you've got it down to a T. . . .

TWICE WASHED

The rain rang on the old tin roof as though it was determined to break in. Occasionally, hail would back its racket. I pulled the quilt up under my chin and drifted off into a peaceful sleep, being lullabied by the song of the tin-top tune.

Bill Gerald and I had been friends a long time and had one significant thing in common—a love for his mama's left-handed biscuits. At dawn, she'd call us to come eat them with jars of homemade huckleberry jam and mayhaw jelly. We'd crawl out of those feather beds, go out on the porch, draw us a bucket of water, and wash in a granite basin. Then we'd make a run to the barn—since there was no indoor bathroom—then back to the kitchen, only to be stopped by Myrt's "Have you been to the barn look?" Then back to the granite pan for another rinsing before we got to sit at the kitchen table. We'd bow our heads and wait for the blessing.

Myrt was a widow, but she was some kind of a mama and even more of a human. She could just hold it together, no matter the situation. We never heard her complain, and never ever saw her cry; she was always laughing, raising her three kids without a fuss.

This morning, after we got up and enjoyed our biscuits, we teamed up to milk the goats and cows, slop the hogs, feed the chickens and so on so that we could go and frolic. The rain had stopped sometime during the night, but by the time we got through with our duties, the rain began again. We scurried to the house and the coal oil lanterns had lit up the kitchen where Myrt was singing a hymn, cleaning mustard greens for dinner. You could smell the smoked pork boiling in the pot, waiting for the tender greens. Bill and his brother Bruce and I came in griping because we weren't going to get to play. We were greeted by a box of dominoes that Myrt had set out on the kitchen table by one of the lanterns. She never said a word, just jerked her thumb at the box, and we were soon lost in a new direction.

About three hours had passed before we realized it. The rain was even heavier. We heard a car driving up and we all ran to the door. It was Almeda Hare, Myrt's sister-in-law, and wherever she went, she toted sunshine in her grin. She played a piano by ear and could play a rinky-dink style that would make the preacher pat his foot. She had her two kids with her, Billy Boy and Peggy. They stomped the rain off on the front porch and were welcomed in.

We set in on her to come play the piano, and for more than half a day we listened to her laugh, play that piano, and sing hymns, with all of us joining in.

I look back over the years at how poor we all were and the trouble we bore, and as I can recall, no one, somehow, ever had to be analyzed or counseled.

Well, the depression must not have been such a depressing thing!

There's a world of difference between being poor and happy and being poor and satisfied.

TEATIME

The Company houses were built on a ridge, all in a row, and on the other side of the boardinghouse there was a small one-bedroom cottage where Emmaline lived. Emma was our keeper. We all belonged to Emma. She kept the kids for all the folks going to funerals, the store, or other grown-up gatherings. She was as black as midnight and could drink "home brew" like it was pump water. But if you needed Emma, she was there.

Papa was working at the United Gas Company plant on the graveyard shift and Mama always packed his supper in the top of the old turkey roaster. She would fix him bowls of peas, beans, corn bread, meat, cake or pie, and a quart of iced tea. I'll never know how he held it all! Then Mama would throw a "cup towel" over the whole thing and Carl would catch one handle and I the other, and up the hill we'd head for Papa.

One night, as we carried Papa's supper, all was still, except for the roar of the plant and the occasional low of a cow or bark of a dog. We were "talking" off the varmints and goblins, being careful not to spill anything. Then it happened.

Out of the darkness came a low moan, as though a ghoul had come forth in the dark of night, searching for its soul. There it was again, only this time more painful, more mournful, lonesome, and flesh crawling. A statue stood on that hill: two boys and a turkey roaster. Short, gasping breaths were coming from each boy. Then again ... UMMMMMMM, OOOOOOO, EEEEEOOOOOOO. Nervous eyes stared into the dark, which was so ebony that it seemed to shine. Only now and then a lightning bug would cut a glowing hole into the night; then dark would flow back in and the moan would come again.

We were afraid to stay, afraid to run. Seconds seemed like days. Then it broke loose: laughter ringing into the night, punctuated with, "Lawd, have mercy, Lawd, have mercy." Emma was behind a black stump, rolling on the ground, laughing her heart out at the Addison boys, who by then had recovered and were lying and saying they knew it was Emma all the time. But Papa didn't have to stir the sugar in his tea. It had already been shaken.

Fear is a strange emotion; sometimes it tucks its tail and runs or rears up on hind legs and fights—it flows either way through the same veins, and ofttimes the hero hides his head and the coward will come out slugging.

SPRUNG TONGUE

It was my turn to roll the old homemade wheelbarrow up to the brine box and pick up the ice. "Casin'head" gas had been piped back and forth through the wooden structure which was filled with salt water, forming the best ice maker ever needed. One of the men, maybe Papa, had made some galvanized cans that we'd fill with water and overnight they'd freeze, so there was always a goodly supply for the families in the Quarters.

Jesse Hare was on duty at the gasoline plant that day, and never a man lived that enjoyed his God or fellow man more. Jess, as his friends called him, or Mr. Jess, as us boys would say, enjoyed pulling pranks on any- and everybody, anytime. I rolled the old barrow up next to the side, where I could hose the can until it would turn the ice loose. Jess walked by and greeted me. When I jumped down, after I had filled the can and lowered it back in place, Jess had his knife opened and had scraped the ice off of the pipe. He said, "Stick your tongue to that pipe and see how cold it is."

Boylike, I did and was immediately frozen to it. I jerked back in pain, seeing the top layer of my tongue staying with the pipe. I recall the pain was as though I had a live coal of fire in my mouth. When I finally freed myself, I ran for the house. Jess was trying to catch up, hollering, "I'm sorry, son, I'm sorry. I wouldn't a done that for nothin' in the world."

I didn't die and I didn't hold a hate for Mr. Jess. I didn't stick my tongue to any more pipes, either. Jess and I were friends by the next day because that was his way.

He lived up past Lock Arbor Baptist Church and drove an old Model T truck. One day, he was headed up the lane by Thunder Road, going home. He called to me, and when I got up close, he grabbed me and said, "I believe I'll jus' take you home with me."

He was holding me down on the seat trying to drive with the other hand. I worked one arm loose, and before he could stop me, I had turned off the engine, snatched the key from the switch, and thrown it as far as I could in the woods. Jess walked home that night and I marked our slate clean. I thought he had too, but we still had a running battle of fun for years, each trying to outdo the other.

Many years later, I was a guest speaker at Lock Arbor, his church, where he had belonged for a lifetime. He walked up and hugged me and asked, "Boy, aren't you lost?"

"No, sir, I'm a Christian," I replied.

His eyes sparkled. Then they glistened with tears as he hugged me again. He stood back and with deep feeling asked my forgiveness for what he had done those many years ago. I hugged the old man gently and said, "Oh, my God, Jess, what hurt me only for a day or two has hurt you over fifty years. I knew you didn't mean me any harm."

Jess died not too long after that meeting, but I feel he died more at peace knowing that I had never hated him.

Sometimes what hurt we do to others hurts us much longer than a temporary pain we inflict through thoughtlessness upon someone else. So be careful! When touching other people's lives, you never know when you might bruise a rose.

Attitude is what changes ordinary people into giants and small towns into metropolises.

SKIN DEEP

We had made us some steering posts out of flat sticks and cross-bars to guide our nail keg hoops. We had gotten so good at rolling them, we could run for a mile down any old dirt path and never once let them die. To let your hoop get away from you, fall over, and die showed you hadn't much hooping behind you.

Bendel and Ed were younger than me, but good friends, and we all had our hoops looking like they'd been chrome plated from steady rolling. We were headed for Springhill Cemetery and met William Prophet, who was an old black man with a Vandyke and who looked like a negative of Prince Albert, for he had a black face and a white beard. William Prophet never worked and no one knew where he came from or where he got his money. He was a well-educated man and could talk about anything with great expertise. He lived in a shack of a house with no conveniences and, of course, was of great interest and mystery to us boys.

"Howdy, William Prophet," I greeted him.

"Good morning, boys," he replied.

We always called him William Prophet because you weren't supposed to call a black man mister then or shake hands with him, and now that I'm older and look back, I wish I could see him again. I don't think that was his right name, but he picked a good one, for he was a prophet to us boys—he looked like something right out of the Bible. I'd like to shake his hand and say, "Good morning, Mr. Prophet." But we were young, then.

So we rolled our hoops on by, not realizing that we had spoken to another human being.

So, birds of a feather flock, but then, so do men with the same color skin.

No man is an island, but a lot of my friends are country. . . .

39

JOURNEYS

I can't remember where Mama was the time me and Carl and
Betty and Papa went to Homer to see our cousin Stella. She was
one of Uncle Sidney and Aunt Effie's eleven children and we
ourselves had never been to Homer before, so we were real
excited. Stella was married to a feller by the name of Herman
Jones. He was a big'n, looked as though he coulda plowed without a mule.

Papa warned us when we neared the city limits that when we
got there, we'd better break out our manners 'cause it wadn't
going to be no punchin' 'n gigglin' at the table or loud laughing
and running. He had spoiled the trip already and we hadn't
even been to their house yet.

Herman and Stella came out to the car when we drove up and
we got hugged and we hugged back and went on in 'cause Stella
had a big meal all hot and waitin'. Papa was asked to ask the
blessings and he did. When we started eating, I noticed Herman
was just using one hand to eat with and the other was kinda
propped on his leg. I kept on watching him 'til it musta been a
bother, 'cause he asked, "Hey, boy, what you looking at?"

I said, "I just was wondering what was wrong with your left
arm," and followed with, "I have a biscuit in my left hand and a
fork in the other and I figgered if you didn't have nothin'
wrong, you'd be using both hands too."

"No," he answered, "Stella has been teaching me etiquette and
she said you're supposed to have your left hand in your lap while
eating."

Herman must not have been sure of himself yet, 'cause he just
never could get that hand all the way down in his lap. I allus
figgered if God had a wanted you to eat with one hand, he
woulda had one arm growing out of your navel, like an ele-
phant's snout, so all you'd have to do is stuff yourself. 'Course
God knew what He was doing all the time, 'cause it'd take two
hands to cut meat and butter biscuits and things. We sure had a
good time at their house, though. Next day, a neighbor of Stella
and Herman came by and just happened to mention that he was
going down to Mansfield and that was where my grandmother
lived. I was born in Mansfield and me and Carl set up a howl to
go down there with the man.

We arrived in Mansfield that afternoon, jumped out of the car in front of the big old white frame house on Washington Avenue, and headed for the porch. Big Mother met us in the old vacuum hall and gave us a big hug. "Eh, eh, eh," she said, as she allus did say when she hugged us, and Big Mother allus smelled like a grandmother and we hugged her back.

Next morning was Sunday and the church was right acrost the street, and if we didn't get up and go, it would salivate Big Mother. So, we were up scrubbing by the time day broke. We ate a big breakfast of homemade everything, got into single file, marched acrost the street, and took our places in the Weber's Pew.

There was a poor, old deaf woman sitting on the front seat and she used a hearing bugle, and when the preacher would say something, she'd break out her horn and plant it in her ear. When they sang, she just left it on the bench, and when the song leader's mouth moved, it motivated hers. Well, she had a voice that would worm a dog and you could hear her over the Nabor's Trailer whistle down the street, and she sang every verse, no matter what the congregation did. This morning, Mansfield had an out-of-town and known in more'n two towns singer and the church was packed with anticipation and people, some being Christians.

The song leader got up and gave the song the guest would sing and that's all that poor, little old lady needed, for she put down her bugle and looked up the hymn, and when the singer arose, she rose to the occasion. The duet was soon to become a trio, for in the back of the church, her son was rendering a very loud prayer of Jehovah: "STOP HER, STOP HER, FOR GOD'S SAKE. STOP HER."

God jus' let 'er sing her heart out and the preacher got up 'n gave the benediction, 'cause he couldn't a topped that with a two-hour fire and brimstoner.

The days passed fast and me, Carl, Max, Max's brother Bill, and Clincy, my other cousin, romped like five savages. We played cowboys 'n Indians, pirates 'n good guys. Max was always "Señor Gray Mask," 'cause he had a Halloween mask that he'd wear even if he was an Indian. "Chief Big Señor Gray Mask." It took half the game, calling his name.

Me 'n Carl decided we'd better git on home to Swartz, 'n since there was no phone at home 'n we knew we could hitch a ride home quick as a letter, we left the next morning.

Wadn't but about 170 miles and that shouldn't take but a day with the ride we had already caught to Shreveport. When we got to the end of Texas Avenue, the man we'd rode with let us out 'cause he was going on north to Belcher. We walked acrost the Red River Bridge to Bossier City 'n on 'n on 'til it seemed like my fat brother wadn't going to be fat no more. We walked almost to Minden along the Dixie Overland Highway, and then I had to go to the woods. Carl was hollering and saying words that if Papa had heard him, he woulda flogged him for sure. I felt better when I got back to the road, but just knew that when I was gone our ride had passed. But a feller came by in a truck and carried us to Monroe, from where we were obliged to walk almost to Swartz. We were out on the Pelican Highway and almost in sight of the Stubbs-Vinson Road, when we heard Luther, our neighbor, coming. . . .

The duet was still ringing in our ears and we almost didn't hear our ride, but even that poor old deaf lady in Mansfield coulda heard Luther's car 'n we flagged him down.

Wherever you are, whomever you're with, whatever you're doing, be entertained. Don't look for the mistakes of man. Look for his mastering of the majority of words, of music, of the brush, of life, of love. The errors of man may be accepted as normal but never the norm. Enjoy the joy of his being alive. Relish his rights but never his wrongs and you too will be alive!

OBSERVATIONS OF A BOY

W.J. swung his cane back and forth in front of his knees, not unlike the stiff tail on a dog. It was his custom to clear out an area in front of himself so he could spit his tobacco without hitting anybody, for W.J. was blind.

W.J. owned the Red Store Grocery and always had a group of local statesmen, politicians, and financial advisors sitting out front on the low benches. Uncle John and Frank were always there; neither had any families to answer to, no real occupation. Neither had developed a taste for work, so neither indulged in it. They both would have made astute lawyers, for each had attained great talent for confrontations and they argued endlessly. Frank was or pretended to be a little deaf, and John just usually ignored Frank's hand to the ear and puzzled look. John was leaning on Frank pretty heavily about being a hardheaded old bag of wind, who would lie under oath and place truthtelling on the endangered species list. Frank just sat hunkered over, holding his head in his hands. When John finished his long dissertation, Frank looked around and everybody waited for his retort, which wasn't long in coming.

"John, you miserable old infidel. I hope I outlive you for one reason only. I wanta bury you and I'm gonna place you face down in the grave so on resurrection morning, when Gabe blows his horn, you'll just dig deeper and then the whole world will be rid of you."

Frank got up, walked inside, and got himself a cold Jax out of the ice. John had followed him in and asked if beers came only one to a box. Frank either ignored or didn't hear him because he shoved by John and went back to his bench.

Old Gute was walking up the Pelican Highway with his familiar gait and grunted something in German as he passed by the unofficial town meeting. Gute walked over to Uncle Tip and asked for a "cold Chix." He always had trouble saying Jax, but everybody at the store knew what he drank.

Volley Veaux was poking around in the back, looking in a junk heap for bottles someone may have overlooked but usually didn't. Satisfied there was nothing worth his salvaging, he gave the heap a kick and walked off. When Veaux came out by the front, Old Gute hollered at him.

"Hey, Veaux, ya vant a bottle of Chix? A bottle mit somethin' in it, hey?"

Frank looked up, cupped his ear with his hand, and asked, "Eh?"

"I vasn't spoke to you," Gute growled.

John answered Gute by saying, "Yeah, I'll take one."

Gute just shook his head.

Sam Walker drove up in his Model T Ford pickup with a load of crossties he had just hewn. Sam was an artist with a broad axe and could turn out good ties, square and true, and was much in demand. He walked up to the counter and asked for a twist. A twist was really known as a "pig's twist." It was made by rolling leaves of tobacco together and picking it up in the middle, where it would droop down on either side, looking not unlike a huge Manchurian mustache. It was then twisted together and hung up to cure. Sam paid for his tobacco, broke off a quid, put the balance in his overall jumper pocket and rubbed the quid between his palms to crumble it. The he loaded his corncob pipe, struck a match with this thumbnail, and lit up. Mosquito hawks died six feet over Sam's head with the first puff. Everybody backed up from the aroma.

Sam's preacher was riding with him—he sometimes supplemented his meager salary by helping to cut ties. Reverend Jumps had been waiting in the truck, but he decided he needed a pinch of snuff. He reached outside to the door handle, let himself out, and shuffled over to the store, not bothering to lace up or tie his shoes.

"What you need, preacher?" asked the young clerk, Wilson.

"Jus' a little ole nickel can of Levi, please, suh."

Wilson placed the snuff on the counter and asked, "Anything else?"

"Naw, suh." The preacher tamped the can on the counter to settle its contents, then uncapped the Levi, pulled his lower lip out, and tapped the can until he had his pinch. I had been watching these scenes unfold from my perch on an apple box inside the store, without comment, but when the preacher got his snuff, I couldn't resist a gentle admonition of the sins of tobacco.

The old preacher stopped, hooked his thumbs under his overall suspenders, and said, "Sonny, when Gaud created de world,

He walked acrost the earth wearing a ticking sack 'crost His chess and He rotched His hand down in de sack and fetched Hisself a handful of seeds, drawed His arm back, and scattered dem acrost the land. He looks back ova His shoulder at His peoples and says, 'Now, you uses dees as you sees fits.' Well, sonny, I sees fits to dips." He winked, nodded, and shuffled back to the truck. I learned to interpret the Bible. It takes age, sage and our needs or inconsistencies (Living Bible, Matt. 11:16).

Lewis, Cudd, and Jack came roaring up full of their tall tales and other stuff, each trying to outlie the other and each seeming to succeed. Cudd ended it by bragging he'd sold a man a dead cow and his customer was satisfied.

Jack said, "Bull."

Cud said, "No, sir, it was a steer."

Uncle Tip stepped in and said, "Aw, Cudd, why don't you go on and tell 'em. I bought the beef and it's hanging in the cooler. It had to be dead, before we skinned it! Thunder, you three act like a bunch of high school young'ns."

The three got themselves a beer and roared off to stir up some more mischief somewhere down the Pelican.

Ma Perkins came in shaking her head at the three who just sped by her. Ma had a jar in her hand and when she walked in, she slammed it down on the counter and stated, "I want another sack of cornmeal and I don't want no damn weevils in it. I brought you these back to let you know I don't like 'em, don't eat 'em, and don't intend to start this late in life. And I'm here to tell you if there's one weevil in this new sack, I'm going to have somebody's hide."

Tip was agreeing, "Yes, mam, yes, mam," then made a mistake by saying, "We didn't charge nothin' for 'em anyhow," then ducked just as a jar of weevils flew past his head.

Ma Perkins left as she had entered, shaking her head, but toting a new sack of meal.

My brother, Carl, came in and somebody said, "Hey, Dr. Pepper! How you been?"

Carl went over and got himself a Dr. Pepper as everyone knew he would. He wouldn't drink anything else as long as he could, get his Pepper.

W.J. was the police juryman for RFD #3 and he always had Carl drive him—well, most of the time. Of course with W.J.

being blind, Carl had to point out the things W.J. couldn't see, like, there's a ditch that's stopped up or Widder Glass needs some new culverts. Carl didn't have to tell him if a road needed grading, because old W.J. knew every bump and hole in the ward and he'd make a mental note of it and never forget it. W.J. knew everybody by their voice and he'd call you by your first name.

Well, the time drags by on a country day at a country store, but it was nigh four o'clock and in just six hours, the store would be closing. The two old coots out front were still burying each other and digging each other up.

"Hey, Tip, how about a nodder cold Chix?" Gute asked.

"Come git it yourself, you old Kraut." Tip's mustache was bristling, but he had to turn his attention to another customer and he cooled in time.

I got up off my apple crate and started for the door. It was getting toward egg-gathering and milking time. Wilson had started lighting the gaslights as dark started moving into the corners, under counters and the lower shelves.

Dad-blamed cows. It was just getting time for folks to come by the store and things would start picking up but I've got to get chores started. I walked slowly up the Pelican and the dust hung heavy over the gravel road.

I met two or three cars whipping up more dust and heard them turning in at the Red Store, and wished I was older so that I could do what I darn well pleased.

When I started down the hill, I could see Papa out by the barn. He always motivated me by getting to the task at hand first, and I'd feel guilty. I walked through the lot gate and looked toward the calf shed, half-expecting old Bully to rush out at me. Then I remembered that we had had blessings over Bully and my eyes got misty, but just for a moment, because Papa said, "Look alive, boy. Let's get done and I'll play you a game of dominoes."

Papa beat me bad the first two games and said, "Old man, if you don't get your mind off the bunch at the Red Store, you'll lose again."

"Papa, I was just thinking about Jimmy Huskey. He was supposed to bring me some mercury from his well route and if I'm not at the store, he might think I didn't want it. Would you mind if I went back to see if he's there yet?"

"Naw, son, you're not going to be able to play dominoes until you do," Papa replied.

I ran all the way back and met Jimmy coming across the road with the small stone jug about a quarter full of mercury. I'd be the richest boy in the country until we'd use up all my mercury making pennies look like dimes. Then I'd be just another boy looking for a new way to "outcon" the other boys. I went behind the store, hid my new fortune, and hurried back to see the action in the store.

Frank had moved on home and John had moved inside and taken over my box seat, the apple crate. I moved back toward the meat counter and sat on a croaker sack full of spuds and became all eyes and ears.

The conversation had turned to the long, hot dry spell and everybody had suggestions for making it through but nobody had an answer. William Prophet came in with his Vandyke trimmed and smoking a King Edward cigar. He walked over to the tobacco case and waited for someone to wait on him. William's black face glowed in the gaslight, as though he had greased himself.   .

The Red Store was soon to be thrown into a turmoil as was the rest of the neighborhood by the arrival of a fast-moving car that was roaring up Wham Hill, past Lock Arbor Baptist Church, and down by Springhill Cemetery with its horn blowing. It came into sight like a horizontal tornado, with the dust whirling behind as it was flung into animation by the speeding automobile. The whole citizenry of the Red Store ran out to see what all the ruckus was about.

With rocks flying and brakes squealing, the driver stopped and gently helped a pregnant woman out of the car. Then he ran up to the closest house, which was Raymond Swanson's. Mrs. Swanson stood only for a moment in the doorway and beckoned the two to enter. After a short passing of time, the man came out to his car and cranked the engine and left. Raymond came walking over to the store and put our curiosity to rest.

Mr. and Mrs. Swanson had come down South from Pennsylvania and were a credit to Dixie. Raymond said Mr. Conger from Oak Ridge had been taking his wife to Monroe to have a baby but the little miss just decided to be born at Swartz at the Swansons'. That was the second time that day the Swansons' house would cause note. Why, just that morning, a bloodcur-dling scream had come from their house and the whole Quar-ters had converged on the source to see what or who was being murdered. It was just Mrs. Swanson carrying out her self-made promise. She had bought ninety yards of muslin to make drapes and it was forever more a chore. She had sworn if she ever got it done, she was going to scream. Now, Lena Swanson doesn't lie and when she'd sewed the last stitch, she let out a bellow that would make a banshee blush.

Well, that morning and then that night they just had to win the "awaken the neighborhood award."

William Prophet was back at the tobacco case when the crowd returned to their respective roles of being poor.

Tip picked up a nickel's worth of cigars and gave them to William and asked, "Anything else?"

"No, suh, but thank you." William lit up a stogie and walked over to the drink chest, dug through the ice, and pulled out a bottle of Bud. William took a long drag and said, "Ahhh, the bitter sweetness of a cold beer. S'cuse me, gentlemen, and good night."

The evening was coming to a close. It was almost 9:45 and Papa was sure to be waiting to give me old billy-be-dad-gum for hanging out at the store. Gute had downed over a case of "Chix" and was making steady trips out back. Uncle John was asleep sitting out by the door. The Swansons' house was growing quiet; the night noises were growing loud. I got up off the spuds, stretched, and started home. Missing the next fifteen minutes would be easier than listening to Papa for thirty. I was just past the land on the east side of Burkholders when I noticed two men in the middle of the road. The night was so dark they didn't even notice me and I didn't speak. I never knew who it was or what they wanted or anything. I just slipped on by them and ran like the devil. I figured it must have been somebody bad. Any-how, they got me home sooner than I'd figured but not soon enough.

I could see Papa sitting by the radio, with his paper crumpled in his lap, resting his eyes. If I could just slip around back and peel off, I could get into bed without him even knowing what time I'd come in. Well, sir, just as I got into that feather bed, I heard him ask, "You in bed yet, old man?"

"Yes, sir," I called, feigning sleepiness.

"Did you see those two men on the road, son?" he asked.

"Yes, sir."

"Well, they passed a couple of minutes ago and I was just wondering if you'd seen 'em on the way home."

"Yes, sir," I said.   Caught again. "Good night, Papa," I said.

"Good night, old man."

And I rested my eyes.

One positive side of my becoming old is, if the same topic comes up again tomorrow it will be a refreshingly new conversation.

STILL AFLOAT

The swamp was quiet, except for an occasional disturbance of the leaves as a breeze would gently move, or a wood duck's squeal as it cried in anticipation of the company of another of its kind. The smoke from the floating still was rising straight up through the cypress trees at the break of morning. A fog hung onto the marsh as long as possible and only turned loose when the sun warmed the surface of Chauvin, letting it rise above the murky waters.

The still was the result of ingenious planning. Built entirely on a log float that could be pulled to different locations, it prevented the fire tower ranger from finding and reporting the cause of the smoke and then having some "revenooer" shut down the draw.

This morning, the bootlegger was smiling as he tied a line from the still to a cypress shoot, then walked to the opposite corner of the float and secured it to another tree. He was certain he was alone to mind his "makin's" in peace. Next, he checked the thump rod and heard the steam moving. He pulled a *Wild West Weekly* out of his hip pocket, pulled a cowhide chair over to the boiler, leaned back, and began to read about a fictitious stampede of Texas long-horned cattle.

Gene Willis was a "well rider" in those days for a gas company and had to use a boat to check the wells in Chauvin. It was a daily affair to change the charts, wind the clocks, and fill the pens with ink so the day's production could be recorded. Then he checked for leaks or any other malfunctions.

Gene was paddling along silently, watching wildlife stirring in their fluid habitat, and the moonshiner was lost in the rough country of the West in his weekly. The whiskey-maker was unaware that he had chosen a site right smack in the path of the chart-checker.

Gene first heard the "blump, blurp, blump, blump" of the boiler, as it brought the good of the grain to a rolling boil. Putting his paddle aside, he started moving his boat through the swamp by pulling from tree to tree with quiet care. To his right and not aware of his newly arrived company sat the bootlegger.

Gene picked up his paddle, and when his boat was about

twenty feet from the barge, he slapped the surface of the water with his oar and hollered, "Get 'em up!"

The events that followed were sheer chaos. Up jumped the reader, losing his place, knocking over his chair, and slapping his hat off as he reached for the sky! Gene almost fell out of his boat laughing and by the time he recovered his composure, his captive had regained his and was holding the biggest musket barrel on Gene's nose.

Gene said, "Put that damn thing down and gimme a drink!"

The whiskey-maker had recuperated enough by then to grin a little. He held out the gun to give his finder a steady hand aboard and both proceeded to sample the dripping of 200-proof brew and 100-proof inebriation. Within an hour, a deaf, blind revenuer could have found them by their raucous laughter and all-day singing, which was a cappella but without harmony. There was an exodus of all wild things from that area of Chauvin and many seasons would pass while the Department of Wildlife and Fisheries wondered at the cause of this sudden departure. . . .

The simple formula is "Men Plus Mash = Mass Migration."

Some people are so negative all the time it's the only thing they're positive of!

RED

Old Red was a muscular dog and not of any definite background, save for a bunch of gregarious ancestors, some of whom must have fought with wolves or worse. Fear was not known by Red. He would tackle anything, anytime, anywhere. Red didn't belong to me; he belonged to my buddy, Sidney, and that was almost like being mine. But he never stayed at my house unless Sid stayed. Then he'd be right at home.

One day, Sid and I were hunting down near Lafourche Swamp and a big cat was following us. We never could get a shot at it and Old Red was way out front on a hot trail, being some kind of a hardhead to give up, no matter how Sid called. We were getting spooked, and still no clear shot and still no Red. We climbed a tree hoping we could get some sight of the cat, but it was like a ghost in the tall palmettos. All we could hear were its snarls.

Suddenly a red blur charged out of nowhere—a slashing, growling, killing machine. Old Red was magnificent and the cat was vanquished. We climbed out of our tree and felt safe again.

One Saturday, Sid, his brother Cliff, and I were walking toward my house and Old Red was clearing the way, scouting the point and stopping to look over his shoulder to see if we were approving. Old Red climbed the railroad bed and stood with feet planted firm. We could hear the train coming, but Old Red had already heard it and the hair bristled on his back as he showed his fangs and warned the oncoming train that it was in danger of one whale of a fight. Red stood his ground, with Sid, Cliff, and me screaming at him to no avail. The train was like a mountain bearing down on him. At the last moment, Old Red realized he could not fight this monster of steel and turned to run. The engine was upon him in a second and Old Red was no more.

We did not go across the railroad track there for a long time and that day we did not play.

It's hard to shoot marbles or do anything that's fun when you can't see through tears.

The loss of a friend is much more costly than the loss of an argument.

VISITATION

Us white boys decided we'd amble down to Burk's Quarters and go to church. It was just a little old unpainted wooden building, set on sawed-off billets, with a tin roof. The old preacher was as black as midnight with a voice that filled every crook and cranny in the place, 'cause even when he whispered, us and God all heard him good.

I was ten or eleven, as were the rest of this adventurous bunch of boys, and we were all set to have some fun with the whole congregation. We eased in the door so as not to make any noise but the rusty old hinges sounded like a flock of guineas had been scared off their roosts!

The old preacher peeped over his specs at us and never slacked. I looked all around at the insides of that small building—homemade pews, rough-built pulpit, no piano, not one hymnal in sight. The resonant voice of the old gentleman gleaned from a tattered Bible, ". . . man's born of woman, life's full of trouble and woe," then the whole place was caught up in an old spiritual. Their voices harmonized together in a plaintive plea to their Maker. No one tried to outsing the other, yet each one, in their own style, blended together like a bouquet of flowers.

Us boys looked at each other, wide-eyed and silent, filled with awe and at the same time hoping they would not guess we had come as the devil's disciples to disrupt their worship. I was jarred back to reality by the old preacher's lone voice saying, "Let us pray."

I was trying to figger out a way to git outa there 'fore he finished, yet I sure didn't wanta scare them guineas again!

"We thanks Ya for all Yoah goodness," the old preacher went on, "Yoah love, and we ask Ya to bless us all, these young white boys and their folks, too."

I was some nervous and my buddies were as fidgety as a long-tailed cat in a room full of rockers. I missed most of the benediction, trying to see a hole to run to. We heard him say "Amen" and the wad of us hit the door running. We didn't slow down 'til we passed Ramsey's house.

We ran up in the woods off the old gravel road and sat in the dark, expecting God to git us.

53

Lavelle finally spoke up and said, "Man, I never thought it'd be like that!"

"Me neither," some voice said shakily in the dark. "Evah one of 'em musta been eight foot tall!"

"Well, I'll bound you one thing," Burton chimed in. "I ain't nevah gonna mess with nobody's church agin, not nevah!"

"Me neither," vowed Shaky.

"Did you evah hear such? Man, that preacher's voice sounded like he done met God hisself!" spoke up another night-flighter.

"Ya know who he is, don't ya? He heps old Sam Walker cut crossties foah a livin'," I spoke up, still out of breath.

"Ya know somethin' else? What surprised me was they's praying to the same God Papa prays to and he's a deacon!" Warren added to the council.

"I know 'nother thing, too," Clyde countered. "I nevah had my plans changed as quick as lightning 'fore. Shucks, I thought we was gonna spook their meetin' but they fair more showed us. Lawd a mercy, I'm still ashakin'!"

"One thing for shore," Sid stated simply. "If Papa evah hears I went to church, without a threat, and the mischief we was gonna do, he's gonna whup my britches off."

"Mine, too," said Shaky.

So many years ago, still I remember that night as though it were last eve and I learned:

No man has a monopoly on God, no man.

It will take more than the "change" in your life for you to be a true tither to God.

IT'S ONLY MAKE-BELIEVE

There was an old riverman called Henry in our community who made whiskey. Everybody knew it, but nobody would turn him in because the drunks were faithful and the sobers never knew when they'd get "snake-bit." So he operated in reasonable safety.

Birds and beasts were permanent tenants of his, or they had accustomed themselves to the delicious spillage which they light-headedly preferred over the local creek waters. Everything was in idyllic suspension . . . the aroma of the still attracted more and more of the keen noses of animals and the booze-hungry beaks of birds.

Then, the inevitable happened. A myna bird owned by the local newcomer was caught up in the caravan to the clandestine cauldron and the fowl imbibed too much, too soon. His owner, mystified by the bird's thick-tongued utterances, followed the next flight and caught Henry in the act of drawing off a batch.

The newcomer hit upon the idea that he would pretend to be an investigator for the U.S. government, and as such he presented himself to Henry. He arrested the whiskey-maker and confiscated his last draw. After they loaded the wooden kegs of booze aboard his Model A, he bid his prisoner to sit up front beside him and away they went.

The Model A cleared the woods and Henry was begging to be turned loose. So the investigator told him that if he kept his mouth shut and promised not to make anymore whiskey, he would release him.

Old Henry had his hat in his hand and was showing what was left of his teeth, mumbling, "Thank you, suh, thank you, suh."

The man from back East drove off laughing about the free booze he had acquired. He could hardly wait until he popped the bung and drank some of the homegrown whiskey. He drew the clear liquid into a cup and with great anticipation dragged deeply, only to discover this keg was filled with water. The rest were too. So as not to have a total loss, he drank from the kegs of make-believe whiskey and got on a make-believe drunk. He shot the myna bird and made-believe it was a pheasant.

But afterwards, the thief could never drink water without having a hangover.

To avoid being owed an apology, never be affronted.

TOEING THE LINE

We had all of our favorite marbles in the ring, because today we were playing for "keeps." We knew it was sinning 'cause the preacher had said it was gambling any way you cut it. Well, we had played "bound you" long enough. This was for keeps.

All us boys who were going to play took our places across a drawn line, policing each other so's we wouldn't fudge across the mark. We started throwing our favorite breaking taws at another line. We called it "lagging." Whoever got closest was first and then on and on as you lagged.

While we were busy taking minute measurements, some of the larger boys came charging around the schoolhouse and scooped up our ring full of marbles, shouting "razoo" and taking off in every direction. All of us had lost more marbles to these pirates than we had ever lost playing for keeps.

I have often thought of those days and the lesson I had learned. If you don't want to be known as someone who has lost their marbles, "keeps" them in your pocket.

Everyone is aware the hen has produced an egg upon hearing her proud cackling. However, very little credibility would have been lent to the occasion should she have crowed; or as we would say at RFD #3— just because you're making a big fuss about something doesn't mean you're telling it like it is!

NO CLAIM IN THE WOODS

Wham Hill was appropriately named, especially in its infancy, for it's a steep incline with a railroad crossing at the bottom. And before hard-surface roads, it was a greased-lightning sliding ramp for beasts, autos, 'n buckboard wagons alike. When it rained, you'd better check the train schedule 'n stay clear because if the local was coming 'n you were headed down, you realized just before you had a tie with the engineer that it was gonna be "wham!"

When Papa would get to the hill headed up, he'd turn the old T Model 'round 'n back up to keep the gasoline flowing to the carburetor. It was a funny sight when you met someone coming down and you were going up, and both of you were pointed in the same direction.

One morning, we went squirrel hunting and Sonny Burney and his Pa went with us or us with them. We rode in the rumble seat, me, Carl, and Sonny.

Papa had a double-barrel shotgun 'n he could shoot it like a rifle. All of us had a single shot—'cept Mr. Burney, he had a pump. Well, you just learned to point better with a one shot and wadn't so set to close your eyes when you pulled the trigger. With a box of Ward's Red Heads costing seventy-two cents for twenty-eight, a body wadn't allowed any seconds, so you looked right at what you was shootin' and if you knocked it down, you jumped on it like a "yonder it goes." (A "yonder it goes" was so fast that you never did have a chance to say "here it comes.")

Papa had killed more in time and Mr. Burney had bagged three or four bushy tails, too, and us boys were just messin' 'round. We heard a crack of a rifle and drifted in that direction to discover a big, fat hog somebody had shot and when they heard us coming, they'd run. Seemed a shame anybody'd kill a fat hog, then hafta leave it, 'cause we wouldn't a touched it with a ten-foot pole, 'cept if we had a claim in the woods.

We walked in a big circle around that dead pig and looked at the other hogs watching nervously. They knew something was amiss but didn't have sense enough to run off and hide from the problem, which coulda been us. We called off the dogs 'n got 'em busy working the pin oak flats and some bitter pecans that had telltale cuttings under 'em where the squirrels had been feeding without disturbance 'til now.

We all got us a bait of hunting and decided to call it quits. We loaded up the T and headed for the house for groceries. We backed up Wham Hill, turned around, and made a beeline to the hive. We hadn't been away from the house more'n three hours and it was about 8:30 when we divided the kill. Mama was out on the veranda inviting everyone to make haste and wash 'cause she had biscuits big as cat heads ready for the baking. She would have us all a batch of yard eggs fried soon as the bacon caught up with the "cat heads." The dad-gummed cows were lowing their fool heads off and milking was a chore to be done before I sopped one egg. I grabbed the bucket, drew me some water, and bellered back at 'em, "I'm acomin', I'm acomin'." I milked like I was possessed and let the calves in while Papa and Mr. Burney skinned and washed the squirrels. Mama set the table, Papa said the blessin's, and we all got down to business.

Saturday wadn't even tapped good and most the chores were behind us, 'cept sweeping the yard. Our yard looked like chickens lived there, 'cause there never grew a blade of grass that didn't get picked and I bet I personally wore out a hundred switch-cane brooms. Swish, whish, swish, whish. If you stopped, Papa could tell right away, 'cause nothin' sounded like a cane broom, unless it was a wet corncob acomin', but it didn't sting as bad as Papa when he got you back to sweepin'. Carl and me made short work of the yard cleaning and headed for Long Bridge Creek.

The snakes and turtles would be checking the weather by sticking their heads out of the water and we'd skip rocks at 'em. We never hit a one, but we had 'em ducking. We both jus' happened to fall in so we mud-crawled in our clothes for about an hour. Paul Quinn, the Reeveas brothers, Clyde Poole, the O'Neal boys, and a bunch of others were down in the gum thicket hollering, whooping, and acting like savages. We mosied over and it wadn't anytime 'til we were soon choosing up sides to play deer and dogs. Carl and Paul led one group that quit and left, but me and Sid had our dogs out loose and hot on the trail, running north of the Pelican Highway behind the Rollinsons' place. We hadn't seen the deer since they left the gum grove but we wouldn't give up 'til we caught 'em. Robert and Burton were the deer and both knew the woods, so they wouldn't be easy caught. By now it musta been near three o'clock 'cause the whistle at the plant had blown noon a long time ago and we were getting more interested in eatin' than catching the deer. We could hear the chickens cackling at the Mosely house, so we knew we'd run several miles without stopping.

Somebody ran across the drove of wild ducks that for some reason wouldn't fly, even with all us circling 'round 'em, hollering and waving clubs and sticks and things. We were going to have duck for dinner and Calvin Reeveas was going to see to it. He was left-handed and had an L-shaped pine knot that was as deadly as a double-barrel. We rustled up a match and some of us gathered wood, while the pickers cleaned the fowl and hacked it up in chunks. We all cut us some switches, sharpened them to spear the meat, and then burned it over a pine-knot fire. The first bite was enough to prove turpentined duck wadn't never gonna catch on, 'less you were trying to show your buddies you could eat anything and they wished you'd quit so they could quit, too.

Well, sir, we were saved from a life of sin by old Mutt Mosely, who came charging into our dinner on the ground. He was screechin' and hollerin', "Them there's my ducks and every last one of y'all gonna pay me or I'll see ya freeze in hell." Man, I just thought I'd been chasin' deer. I'se runnin' 'fore I got up and my overalls bloomered out with air like as though I'd been pumped up! I run a mile in the wrong direction 'fore I got my senses. Mutt caught Sid, Cliff, and six others, one of 'em being Clyde. He took 'em, each one of 'em, to their papas and demanded a dollar apiece. He couldn't a got two bits for that duck but he sold that little ole biddy thing for eight dollars. 'Sides that, Mr. Bob, Sid's pa, killed his boys' taste for duck forever more, even if you'd give 'em one.

Papa never did find out, which in the long run was worse 'cause 'em other boys got over theirs by 'n by, but my sufferin' was strung out forever jus' waitin' for Papa to ask me how to cook a duck.

Some were caught, but all of us were marked, for even today when I go duck hunting, before I shoot I look around for Mutt or Calvin.

In building character one should remember that if you ever do anything distasteful for the first time, it will be last time you'll ever be able to say, "I've never done that."

LONG-HANDLED AND LONG GONE

Long-handle underwear has gone by the way of coal-burning locomotives, almost into a big roundhouse in the sky. Aw, you see hunters, lumberjacks, and some outdoor employees wearing them, but usta be everybody that walked wore 'em.

Wool, flannel, cotton, knit—some had a slit down the back with one button, some had a trapdoor sporting three buttons across the top, and some really fancy kinds had elastic in the top. But, they were pretty risky!

One thing I remember is, if you were bowlegged, your long-handles were bowlegged hanging on the line—if you were knock-kneed, the same. They took on the characteristics of their wearer, good or bad.

People used to sleep in 'em, just like they were pajamas. Personally, I never slept in pajamas until I was grown and gone from home. Come to think of it, I never slept between sheets until I was a senior in high school and spent the night with C. G. Pearce. Sometime during the night, I woke up at his house and thought I had been called home and was wrapped in a heavenly robe.

One year, when spring was trying to break in line with winter, the Louisiana weather was giving an example of all four seasons in four days running. Cold, hot, sleet, sweat, short sleeves, overcoat—just hang in there, a change would come in the climate. I recall one day in early spring when morning arrived with a killing frost. Everybody's folks got up threatenin' a dose of calomel to all who didn't wear their "longies" to school. You had to protect yourself in this weather from gettin' holes all through your insides, which they called "being salivated." Just as sure as dirt, it'd be hotter'n the hinges of Hades before school let out— but 'at didn't matter. You'd wear 'em suckers before you'd take that chance of being salivated.

We wadn't disappointed, 'cause it was a sweatin', sittin'-still kinda day.

Allus kids didn't wait for the school bus; we just started walking home down the railroad track. One girl, and I ain't gonna never call her name, had rolled her long handles up and her long stockings down so's not to be so hot 'n bothered as she walked. Well now, I don't care if you're a graduate of Sophie

Newcomb, you can't walk on railroad ties without jarring your gizzard out. As she walked along, the constant uneven gait caused her rolled-up flannel union suit to slither down her leg like the open end of a croaker sack as though it was trying to eat her feet, 'cause she'd rolled 'em up so many times before, they'd lost their shape and looked like she'd got 'em from somebody with the milk leg.

She turned redder'n a rooster's comb and lit a shuck down that railroad track and the last time I seen 'er, she's crossin' the trestle and Hancock's Spur with a full head of steam. I swear on a clear night in spring, you can still see her flaggin' by, with 'er long handles flapping, redder'n a fox's fanny at pokeberry time. I bet if she had a second chance, she'd as soon have been salivated or sweated her heart out in her flannel sauna bath.

We didn't time her but I believe she would have won the blue ribbon any day of the week in a dead heat.

When you have to do without something long enough, you learn to do with. . . .

63

CHASING DREAMS

Papa had built a small fire to kill the spring chill and I was sitting spraddle-legged close to the flame with a pair of pliers, a thin nail, and a piece of copper wire that I had unwound from an old electric motor. My shoes had split up the back—just old, cheap shoes that had come apart and I had been walking around with claw toes holding them on my feet. But they were my school shoes and I wasn't the only one in the family, so, I made do. . . .

Holding the nail in the fire with the pliers until it got red with heat, and then burning holes in the leather on both sides of the slit made lacing it up with copper wire a neat repair. At least I could run again without losing my brogans.

I made the last lace and twisted the copper together when I heard someone holler, "School bus, school bus a'comin'."

No one at school noticed my shoes or cared, or if they did, they didn't say. Almost everybody was poor. We had been exposed to the depression from every angle and we never did develop a taste for being needy.

The day was uneventful, one hour stacked on another until it was time to head for RFD #3 again. I hopped off the bus, ran into the house, changed clothes, kicked off my new copper-toned shoes, and grabbed a biscuit. The weather was warm enough to go barefoot in the late of the day and no day passed that I didn't take advantage of the freedom from being shod.

Every afternoon my brother, Carl, delivered the evening paper and he'd made a deal with me to deliver "Ma" Perkins' daily news for a nickel a trip. The Perkinses lived up on a hill overlooking Long Bridge Creek to the one side and Springhill Creek to the other. The distance in a straight line was hardly enough to get up a sweat, but picking a way to outguess the Murphy boys made the journey six times longer. The Murphys lived up Springhill Road and the three I had to outrun were James, Bill, and Dickie. They were so tough that when they got sick, they wouldn't even have fever.

James was about my size and age and the ringleader. He led his pack like a general, up and down the ravines, around the buckeyes and briar patches, a relentless pursuer of his prey.

When I crossed the pipeline right-of-way, they saw me and I saw them. I ran into the woods and instead of heading toward the Perkins' house, I ran in the direction I had last seen James. I stopped after a while and lay still. I could hear James shouting at his brothers to cut me off at the Ritchies'. After a short time, I could no longer hear their voices, so I eased along until I was just inside the woods south of the old gravel road. When I got within about two hundred feet from the Perkins' front porch, I climbed a stubby oak, so as to survey the field of fire and try to see the Murphys. They were nowhere in sight, so I climbed down and made a beeline for the Perkins' porch. I didn't slow down as I made a looping throw on the run. I knew I had hit something wrong, because I heard "Ma" Perkins swearing. She was so good at cussing, she could peel bark off a tree at a hundred feet and across the creek and never get off her porch. I never saw her do it, but I heard tell she could make a hen molt new feathers any day in the week.

Well, when "Ma" commenced to cussing, the Murphys knew I had made my delivery and was headed home. I could hear them behind me but by then I was fairly flying, and when I hit the cow lot gate I just floated through without ever looking back. I slowed to a walk and went on in the house. Once inside, I looked out and all three were grinning and shaking their fists at me, but they couldn't see me or see me grinning back.

Every day was the same—run, dodge, hide, run, hide—I never worked so hard for money in my life, but thirty cents a week wasn't to be sneezed at.

One day, I had made my run, delivered the paper, and hadn't seen hide or hair of them. So, I thought I had it made. But they had outsmarted me by lying in wait. I was about halfway home when James and his brothers came screeching out of the buckeyes. I "lit a shuck" but I couldn't outrun them that day. I'd have to fight. James knew it, too; he'd brought his two-year-old brother, Jackie, with him. He knew he had me cornered. Well, we fought, grabbed, wrestled, and rolled all over the woods, me in desperation and James just grinning and enjoying the melee. We both fought ourselves out with nobody joining in, just sitting there watching me and James. One thing was understood: if James whipped me, the next in line got me on the next catch. But James and I were a match, and after the fight we got up, washed our bloody noses and bruised lips in the creek, and walked together down the pipeline, James toting Jackie on his shoulders. When we got to our back gate, I turned and James grinned at me. I said, "See y'all tomorrow."

When I got to the porch, I turned and all four waved at me. James and I never fought again, nor I with any of his brothers.

I knew then that they did not dislike me. It was the chase. I could have been a dog, a wild animal, or anything. I was a part of their game of life.

The Murphy boys loved a chase, even if it was just a dream. Some of our dreams came true.

Time will not cease, nor has it ever—it runs out on people, but it will never run out. Only someone else will use it more wisely or with complete abandon.

RIDIN' THE RUNNING BOARDS

The first meeting we had to start our Boy Scout Troop out at Swartz was almost the last. We was told how much fun it's gonna be, learning how to build fires, spending the night in the woods, learning how to shoot, how to know different animal tracks, what wild things was good to eat—nothing new, jus' the same old things we'd been doing out at RFD all our lives.

We got our gang together and decided to name our troop the "Grinning Possums Troop #2." We knew we were the first, but heck, we thought #2 sounded like it was older. Some of the bunch built a cage and we caught us a mascot to go with our troop name. It was a scruffy beast, ears almost chewed off, scarred on every side, but it was ours and we named it Smiley.

All of us took a vote and decided to meet two more times to see if they had something else to offer us besides the first gathering. Durn, who wanted to learn how to cook in the woods—we wanted to know how to get hold of some cornflakes. When the meeting was over, me 'n Paul caught us a ride with the Eubanks. Their car was full so we jus' hooked our arms 'round the door posts and rode on the running boards. Our hair was thick with dust and full of lightning bugs and other night fliers by the time we got home, but a good dousing under the pitcher pump gave us a new and cleaner outlook.

Next morning, we were gonna meet at Guy's store 'n talk over our decision. Loy was sitting on the square red box where the bread man left the fresh baked loaves before daylight. Nobody ever stole any of it but the safety of the deposit was to keep some thieving dog honest.

We were milling around, hot and sweaty, with dirt beads on our necks and our clothes clinging to us like a scared child to its mama. All of us was broke and dry as a powder keg. Loy let us all get in hearing distance and with a loud voice called out to Mr. Guy, "I believe I'll have another one of 'em R.C. Colas, please."

Well, that did it! One was enough and here he was hollering for another one. The whole bunch of us almost forgot what we had come up here for. There wasn't a nickel among us boys and old Loy was spending a whole dime drinking two R.C.'s.

It was hard not to be covetous as thirsty as we were but Mr. Guy broke the spell by busting Loy's ploy when he replied, "That'll be a nickel, since it's your first one." We decided on one more meeting to see if we wanted to join the Scouts or just keep on being a disorganized resemblance of a tribe.

Orenay Woods picked up an old cardboard box and started ruling off lines and soon had a checkerboard made. We all began picking up Coke caps and cream soda tops until we had enough men to get up a game.

Sid beat all us, 'n we declared him champ. Somebody pried the cork out of a Coke top with his pocketknife, and we put the metal on the outside of his shirt and pressed the cork back in on the inside and gave him a badge. In one wad, we all headed for the trestle to chunk rocks at turtles 'n snakes.

Cliff stepped on a scorpion and you coulda heard 'im holler over thunder. His foot swole up and we toted him halfway home. Sid got a pint of coal oil and we soaked ole Cliff's foot in it 'n pumped water on his head. All the time Cliff was kicking 'n bellering 'n enjoying all the attention. We propped ole Cliff up by the climbing tree 'n started a game of tin can shinny or bruise your buddy with a broom handle.

Wadn't no time 'n Cliff was up 'n swattin' the short Pet milk can with a stick, 'n 'fore long he was headin' the pack. 'Course he was always a fast healer.

The next week drug on 'n on 'n on but we still talked amongst ourselves about our next get-together. Then it came to a wheel-locking, brake-screeching halt. Old Burton said he'd eaten our mascot! We ran 'n checked old Smiley's cage 'n sure enough, it was empty as a tomb! We asked 'im how come he'd gone 'n done it? He jus' stood there grinning, playing possum on us, with grease all over his mouth.

Oh well, we didn't figger we'd make good Boy Scouts anyhow. None of us looked so proper in our cutoff overall uniforms, anyway.

That weekend we spent two fun-filled days on Panther Lake, catching fish, cookin' and eatin' 'em with onions and french fries, and wishing we lived in town so we could have cornflakes and own us a real Scout knife 'stead of jus' an old barlow.

So ends the saga of the Scouts of Swartz. Except our fate was better than old Smiley's demise, which was nothing to laugh about.

It's not the race I mind in the "rat race," it's the rats. . . .

BEAT'CHA HOME
It Was Winner Take All

Bob O'Neal and Papa had a lot in common. One thing was, if you stayed over night at either of their houses, you belonged to 'em. You were welcome but you became their child—loved, fed, washed, disciplined, jus' like the rest, jus' like at home.

If I was at Sid's house and "Mr. Bob" told us to hush and go to sleep, he didn't "lick his calf but once" and if you didn't get the message straight, he'd come in that dark room and whup everything he caught—didn't matter who. If he laid a hand on you, he laid it on! Same with Papa. If he caught you, he skinned you—even Cliff, Sid's younger brother, got his share. He was the one who could never whisper and even if we meant to get still, Cliff would beller out something and the trap would spring.

Me and Sid were allus good buddies, even closer than brothers, 'cause we never fought each other but we fought for each other. We allus made a lot of plans. We were going to join the French Foreign Legion once, or be gamblers on a Mississippi riverboat. We did get around to hunting together, and playing tin can shinny and deer and dog. As it usually happens, we didn't get a bunch of things done we wanted to, but we were still buddies.

We shared muscadines, fox grapes, huckleberries, crawdad fishing, climbing our favorite oak tree, and taking care of Mona, his little sister, or "Scooter" as we called her. We both had a little sister and soon found they were favorite people of their papas. We were forgiven almost anything 'cept not being mindful of those two little girls.

I never told Sid, but I allus envied him owning Old Red. Best dog in the world, even counting mine, and we both cried when the train outfought 'im. Sid had something else I didn't have nearby and that was an Uncle Frank. 'Course I've already told you about him and Uncle John, who wadn't nobody's uncle, that is, that anybody knew of.

I remember ole Sid allus beat me at playing checkers too, but he kept letting me play him 'til I learned to beat him. Then we let each other play 'til we were even.

One thing I allus remember about Sid's house. They were

never without guinea hens and they kept better watch than the yard dogs. Sometimes, they'd even out-dog Old Red on keeping account of things.

The O'Neal house was at the end of a dirt lane and so was ours, both about the same distance from Thunder Road. Each time we'd get to the turn-off point, we'd cry out "beat'cha home" and then pell-mell, lickety-split, head over heels, we'd try to outrun the other. It didn't matter if you had a wrapped-up foot or nothin'; you didn't get a handicap. It was winner take all and the loser had to pump water for the victor. Seemed to take two hours for the winner to get his thirst quenched. 'Course, first thing you allus had to do was hold your head under the pitcher pump 'fore you filled yourself, but that was the spoils of war.

Summer was allus an endless chase, with fall and winter full of hunting and tracking, 'specially if it snowed. We tracked many a rabbit to the hollow tree and a big, fat cottontail fried just right was a meal of memories.

I had not seen Sid, Cliff, or "Scooter" for a long time, but the other night, the gang got together again. Thoughts about those years were fondly recalled as Cliff, "Scooter," and a host of other friends got to reminiscing and laughing about those good old days.

Someone tugged at my sleeve and asked if I had seen Sid. I said, "No, I never look at my friends in their last repose." For I want to remember Sid at the head of the lane looking back over his shoulder at me with that shy smile and if he could have spoken, he would most likely have said, "Beat'cha home, didn't I?"

A true friendship is not unlike an image reflected in a mirror which is then reflected to another mirror and on into infinity. It does not alter nor magnify what it sees; only does it change it into an endless thing. . . .

"I VANT TO BE HALONE"

Gutenheimer often spent all night and all day in Springhill Cemetery, drinking moonshine out of a quart fruit jar, which made it twice as potent and three times faster, for you inhaled the fumes as well as the booze for an accelerated drunk.

Gute liked drinking in the graveyard because nobody bothered him there. But one time he got drunk with his buddies at somebody's house, and they hung him upside down on the back porch and left him there all day. About eight o'clock that night, one of his cronies remembered where they left him and they weaved their way back to the house.

Gute was still hanging by his heels on a hog's gambling stick. His watch had dropped out of his overalls bib pocket and hung down in front of his nose, which would cause him to be cross-eyed for two weeks. Gute's friends cut him down and propped him up against a #3 washtub—eyes crossed and as red as two burning holes in a blanket, hands heavy from hanging, dizzy from alcohol, not to mention his ten-hour, wrong-side-up position. Gute drew a hand across his damp, loose mouth and muttered, "Vot I neet is a dreenk."

Someone produced a fruit jar of White Lightning and after a long pull, Gute "rared back," hollered a good long German shout with a Southern drawl, and fell off the porch, where he was left to sleep until being awakened by a used washbasin of water hitting him in the face at daybreak. "Goot Himmel!" he sputtered, as he rolled under the porch, disturbing a couple of sleeping shoats that announced their departure from under the old house by squealing and scraping each floor joist with their boney backs. Gute kept rolling until he got to the warm spot were the hogs had lain and dropped off to sleep again.

Noon came and passed. One, two, three o'clock and Gute's snoring could be reckoned to a peckerwood sawmill cutting through a knotty log. Finally, the lady of the house could no longer endure the gruesome noise and poured hot water through the cracks in the floor. Gute roared an obscenity and crawled from beneath the house and headed home.

Gutenheimer stayed in the ditches as much as he stayed in the road, for he wasn't used to being cross-eyed and it just seemed he always followed the wrong eye. It was bad enough that he couldn't see well, but the way he stumbled along, everyone thought he was drunk for the next two weeks when he wasn't.

Gute had sworn off; he hadn't had a drink in thirty-three days and he was bored stiff. He was fed up with the day in, day out, humdrum of living. Well anyway, his eyes had gotten straight again. Friday night was going to be different, though, for Ed had offered to take him night hunting for coons and he loved a good roasted coon with sweet potatoes.

About 6:30, Friday evening, Ed hollered at Gute out by the gate and they were soon crossing the railroad at Hancock's Spur. The night closed in around the two men except for the piercing ray of the carbide light Ed was wearing. Along the edge of Boggy Boeuf, some tall cypress grew and it was a great place to find hungry coons high on the limbs, eating cypress balls.

Ed shined his light around the limbs and soon spotted a fat coon trying to hide his eyes. The hunter cocked his old double-barrel, pulled his cap to the left so the beam would align with the sight of the musket, and took aim. The first shot found its mark and the animal was dead before it hit the leaf-padded ground.

Ed and Gute were moving along the edge, looking for their next prey, when there was a loud shout from behind Ed. "Goot Himmel! Vot vas dot?" When the light was shone on Gute, he was wiping his eyes with his coat sleeves, reeking to high heaven and stumbling blind as he tried to clear his eyes. Then Ed's light found the culprit, who was at that time sighting on Gute again. The old double-barrel was slow to the occasion and before it could be fired, the skunk's mate had zeroed in on the old German and got him "bull's eye" again! "Vell, dot does hit, by yemmy, I'm go back to ouse."

Gute could be smelled as far as you could see him. His wife wouldn't let him sleep in the house and besides he had to bury his clothes and scrub with lye soap until he was as pink as a baby. Gute bathed in Long Bridge Creek, but he didn't have a stitch of clothes to wear and he stayed in the water 'til the traffic died down, then ever so cautiously, he slipped out of the water looking like a big, old shriveled pink prune.

"Vell, he yust couldn't stay in de woods all night." So, he slipped along the highway and made a run for the other side just as a car came over the hill. Swartz never was sure who, but did know they had a "streaker" even before it was popular. Gute found a pair of overalls hanging on a neighbor's clothesline and forthwith borrowed them. The clothes were much too small and way too short but they at least covered the embarrassment.

Gute headed for his hidden booze. It was time to go off the wagon. Gute went straight to the hollow tree and pulled out a fruit jar of White Lightning, unscrewed the lid and, as he limped light-footed toward the graveyard, drank greedily from his mason jar. Some local had passed away and a new grave had been dug at Springhill and of course, Gute didn't know it. A light rain had begun to fall and every now and then, a cloud would be lit up with high electricity, just enough to keep Gute on the road, but not enough to keep Gute from preceding the corpse to its last resting place. Gute landed on his head and for a moment he thought, "Vell, I'll be a cross-eyed German again!" After a moment of getting his bearings, he set forth looking for his fruit jar and then tackled the chore of getting out.

The walls of the grave were slick and muddy, and after many unsuccessful tries, Gute decided to "yust vait to morning." So, he sat down and proceeded to empty his fruit jar of booze. Before long, though, one of the boys who lived up Springhill Cemetery Road cut across the graveyard and, without being announced, dropped in on Gute, who by this time was pretty far down in his jug. So, he sat quietly and watched as the new tenant tried to scale the slippery walls. The fellow kept jumping up and falling back, jumping up and falling back, until Gute decided to make known his presence, mumbling, "Vait hey aminit, I giff you a hand." But the new tenant didn't need it and he didn't vait! Gute muttered, "Oh vell, I vanted to dreenk halone hennyvay."

We are being helped by the government to such a degree it's getting to where we can't afford ourselves.

FIDDLING 'ROUND

The fiddle was crying the blues. Old Horace could just naturally handle a bow, but when he played the blues, it was like listenin' to a freight train's lonesome whistle on a cold night. Lord, it was a "by yourself" feeling, a "make you homesick for someplace, empty gut" feeling, a "wipe your eyes, blow your nose" feeling. Make you take a drink is what it'd do.

Then old Horace would play "Sally Gooden" and everybody would start dancing, and even those who couldn't or wouldn't were clapping their hands or patting their feet. It was shameful, said some of the neighbors, and anybody having that kind of fun had to be sinnin'.

Old Horace was playing a "hoedown" now and the bow was as ragged as an urchin. There was enough rosin around the bridge to make a quart of turpentine.

Intermission always was just for four or five minutes, but it sure seemed much longer than the playing. I never did follow the players outside to see what they did, but I heard 'em lotsa times through the window, drinking or something. Anyways, they'd be heard saying, "Augh, whew, hot damn, 'at's hot." Then they'd cough and say, "Gimme 'nother drag."

Most time before the night got old, there'd be more'n one fight and lots of threats and brags but more laughin' 'n dancin' 'n anything else. Nobody had any money to write home about, so you had to go, and if you couldn't dance or play, you had to fight or do something to show you appreciated the hospitality of the host.

The dancers learned to step high because of the rough lumber in the floors and it'd take many a hoedown to wear 'em even smooth moving, but when it came to square dancing, it was just as good as glass. The caller's voice compelled the couples to choose their partners and form a star, and old Horace would bow up over his fiddle like a cutworm and "bile the cabbage down." Dust would fly as they'd swing 'em 'round 'n 'round. Hearts were light tonight, but tomorrow heads would hurt, and in a week everybody would've forgot and get another helping.

A gang of the boys came by and hollered, and me 'n Newty went out to see what was happening. It wadn't nothin' 'cept somebody'd seen old Gute running acrost the road at Long

Bridge Creek, naked as a jaybird. Musta been twenty of us gathered by the time we got to Springhill Cemetery 'n we didn't have to look for Gute any further. He was singing in the graveyard and we homed in on 'im. We were wondering whether to go over to where the singing was coming from, but someone came stumbling up the Pelican 'n cut across the cemetery 'n just dropped out of sight. We woulda gone to help him but whoever it was floated out of that hole 'n cleared the fence 'n disappeared in one direction as fast as we did in the other.

And none of us was fiddling 'round.

The hour we spend "getting ready" to go to work has half the minutes in it as does the last hour "getting ready" to go home. . . .

DEHORNING DRIVER

Carl had been drivin' for over two years and I was a watcher. I wanted to learn how to operate an automobile in the worst way, but I was only thirteen, yet thought I could do anything. 'Course Papa didn't, so I watched.

Our family car at the time was a 1927 Oldsmobile Sedan and was six years old when we got it, but it ran good.

The Swartz Grammar School was having a box supper and a cakewalk to raise money. Horace Goodnight was going to play his fiddle for the occasion and everybody would be there. Carl got the car and reluctantly let me and some of my buddies ride with him.

We could hear Horace's bow talking long before we got there. He was playing a hoedown and getting the folks in a festive mood. The principal had the doors folded back between the fifth and seventh grades. He had a big circle drawn with chalk on the oiled floor with numbers around it and was already selling tickets for the first walk. The music began and the first offering was a five-layer strawberry cake with thick pink icing. The circle began shuffling around with everybody sure they were going to win the first cake. The music stopped, someone drew a number, and a little six-year-old gird squealed but she was on a nine and the number was six. A big red-haired fellow on six stepped forward, picked up his prize, and turned to the little girl, who way cryin'. He said, "Here, sugar, here's your cake." His girl friend looked up at him, smiled, then whispered, "I love you."

"Aw, honey, I'd have choked on that cake remembering her tears," he told 'er.

Horace rosined his bow while folks was getting into the circle for the second walk. All I had was a dime, so I decided I would wait until nearer the end, because they would start giving away two cakes per walk and that would up my odds, and at a nickel a try, maybe I'd get lucky.

The night grew older and I hadn't seen Carl in over two hours, but I didn't concern myself, even if I had to walk home. It wasn't over three miles and I'd run further than that playin' deer and dog, many a day.

The redheaded man had tried several more walks and failed

to win. He and his girl friend walked over to the coffee urn and bought two cups. There was a tug at his sleeve and when he turned, the little girl with the big eyes was holding up two large slices of pink-icing cake. She smiled, curtsied, and ran away without lookin' back.

I heard the principal sayin', "Two cakes per walk, everybody, come on, one and all. Everybody walks, two cakes per walk. Pick a number, two cakes per walk." I mosied forward to take a chance, but all the numbers were gone. The fiddle started again.

I walked the next two times and spent my dime. Oh, well, Mama had a good cake at home.

The bidding was fast on the box lunches, with everyone bidding on their favorite girl's cooking. It didn't matter how it tasted; it was the company that made it eatable.

All us boys hung around until the money was counted and the school had raised about eighty-six dollars. That was more'n any man would earn in a month and a half. A boy came up to me and told me Carl, Drew, and Kirby had driven off in the Maxwells' Model A Ford with some girls, and Carl wanted me to take the car home. I felt like a grown man.

By the time I got the old car started, there was ten or more inside and that many more hanging on the running boards, fenders, or anywhere they could cling.

I was doing fine, slowing down for curves, stoppin' at intersections, and then I turned on the Walker Road, headed for home. I almost made it but a car turned off of the old Monroe-Bastrop Highway with the brightest lights I had ever seen. Sealed beams!

Someone on the right front fender hollered, "Look out for that cow." Heiferlike, she was getting up on her back feet first, and when I saw her she looked as though she was praying. She never finished her prayer, for I ran up over her head, with her bellering and everybody hollering, screaming, and giving directions. I just put the old automobile in reverse and backed off the beast. We rolled her over in the ditch, kicking and moaning, and then we lit a shuck.

The right front light was shining in the trees like I was a moving-on coon hunter, and thoughts were racing through my head. I knew that by morning, the sheriff would come and carry Papa off to prison or worse.

I slept very little that night and by dawn, I was slipping through the woods, a criminal returning to the scene of the crime, to check on the carcass of the cow.

I eased quietly up to the Walker Road, keeping the heavy underbrush between me and visibility, and when I parted the limbs, I was surprised to see the animal gone. I felt a flood of joy, mixed with wonder, spread over me. Papa may not have to go to jail.

I saw Mr. Kinsley out by the barn with a sheet in one hand and a bucket of coal oil in the other. I then saw the cow standing, head up, alive!

Mr. Kinsley wrapped the cow's head in the sheet and poured on the coal oil. The cow just shook her head and limped off.

Mustering up bravery, I walked over and very innocently asked what happened.

Mr. Kinsley said, "Some heathen kids came tearing down the Walker Road and run over my cow."

I told him that I thought it was awful how kids act nowadays, but I was glad his cow was alright.

He said, "Thank you, son, and I appreciate you dehorning her for me."

Right away I headed home.

Counselors call it "due process of the law"—how come in the process many don't get what's due?

WAKE UP IN THE MORNING

Trying to get a job during the depression was no easy matter for a man, much less a boy, but I was gonna try. I caught a ride in from Swartz and got out at the first filling station on the outskirts of Monroe, then stopped at everything that had a Coke sign on it on the way in. I got nothing but experience, tired feet, and about a thousand "no, I don't need ya's."

I was a long way from the house and hungry. The sun had swapped skies with a moon and it was wearing clouds for a shawl. I started for home and before I got out to the Seale Lily place on DeSiard, the dark was moving into every place it could find between the light poles.

I was flagging anything that had a motor running and some fellow stopped and gave me a lift out to Sicard. I walked about five hundred yards or more down the gravel road before I heard a car or truck or something coming, dust boiling over its shadowed back. I was lost in the dirt and rocks wrapping me up, but then it stopped and a horn sounded from within the cloud. I was already dusty anyway, so I just plowed into the middle of it and found an old Ford Roadster with no top and two eyes peering out of a dirty face, grinning at me and asking, "Boy, y'all want a ride 'at's as bad as that there road?"

"Yes, suh," I replied through my mudpack.

We took off in a cyclone that Luther Hoover woulda been proud of, and in no time I was howling over all the noise and sandstorm, "Lemme out about a quarter-mile down the road." When we stopped, we were just past LaDell Hill, so I didn't have to walk but a half a mile or so to get back home.

I never knew who he was or where he was going but when he let me off, you coulda wet him down and sowed a pound of mustard greens on him and never lost a seed. I ain't never seen a man so coated with silt in my life, but he was as fast a ride as you coulda caught.

Papa was sitting in his favorite spot holding his paper in front of him and sound asleep. When I closed the door, he stirred and asked, "That you, old man?"

"Yes, sir."

"You find a job?"

"No, sir."

"Well, don't fret. We'll see tomorrow, and by the way, I d
your chores, son."

"Thanks, Papa," I wearily answered.

Well, I musta been tired, 'cause I didn't wake up 'til 5:30 tl
next morning and I had to get going if I was going to find a jo
It was Friday already, and if I didn't get a "yeah" today, I'd loc
Saturday. Somebody ought to be shorthanded. The odds wei
against me, though, 'cause all the boys from town were lookin
too, and they were just as hungry as me. 'Sides, they were i
walking distance from most jobs.

I finished eating and got me some cardboard and a pencil. I sa
in the old rocker 'cause I could lean forward and press my foc
down hard on the paper and trace each foot. I cut the tracing an
slipped the cardboard into my shoes to cover the holes in th
soles. I pulled at the toes in my socks and folded the holes bac
under, making 'em just like new.

The first car that came by picked me up. It was loaded witl
kids, milk, chickens, and two of the fattest folks I ever laid an ey
on. They were so heavy, their old car looked like it was goin
downhill all the way.

They came all the way to the Community Grocery in Monro
and musta known the man that was boss, 'cause he came out an
hailed them in. I helped them unload their barter and asked th
man if he had an opening in his store for the summer.

"What can you do, boy?" was his first words to me.

"Anything," I replied desperately.

"OK, go check in with the produce department."

I didn't even ask how much I'd make. I had a job!

We worked all day and the store closed at ten o'clock, then w
got the produce ready for Saturday's shopping. It was a littl
after eleven when I started home, but at fifteen cents an hour, 1
was headed to Swartz with $2.10 in my pocket. I would have tc
sleep fast so I could get up and catch somebody coming tc
Monroe—but that was tomorrow. With some fast walking and
three rides, I was ready for a bath and a biscuit when I go
home.

Mama heard me and met me at the door wringing her hands.
"Where in the world you been, Harry Boy?"

"Got me a job, Mama." I went in and sat on the side of the bed
and told Papa about my new job. He was about as proud as I was.

Mama called and I ate two yard eggs, two biscuits, a glass of sweet milk, and headed for bed. I hit that feather bed almost snoring.

The way I had it figgered, by next week, I'd have almost $17.00 and the first thing I was gonna do was get me a pair of shoes. Working in the produce caused my cardboard to give out about noon, and if I didn't get time to put a new one in my shoes, I'd be stepping on rocks in the dark again tonight.

One day followed the next and I handled more turnips, carrots, collards, and the lot than I had ever pulled at RFD #3, but I enjoyed the work. It was great to talk to folks from every walk of life and as shy as I was, I needed the exposure.

Friday noon, I walked around to the Ward's Store and looked at some of the prettiest shoes I'd ever seen, black and brown, from $4.45 down to $1.45. I liked the calfskin black ones. The man said they had French toes, but they were just squared off to me. I finally picked up the brogans for $1.45 because I wadn't the only one that needed shoes at home.

I had an uneasy feeling spending that much money and I was almost hurting when I got my money out to settle up. Then it happened! I spotted a pair of stick-on soles—guaranteed to hold. They were only eight cents a pair! I handed the clerk my coveted new shoes and said, "I'll take these, instead!"

His smile woulda "blue Johned" the milk. That night, I got home about 11:35, 'cause some folks from up close to Lock Arbor Baptist Church were doing some late Friday night shopping and offered me a ride home.

I lay in the bed, hurting from a long day. Saturday was gonna be a busy shopping day, too, but we'd be off on the Sabbath. So, I go to bed tonight, wake up in the morning, and tomorrow will be Sunday.

The great convenience of affluence is you're not burdened by having to think about petty things. . . .

THE WAY I SAW IT THEN . . .

The train whistle cut through the cold winter's air like a long sad sob, like a spinster's sigh. I sometimes believed those old engineers were writing lonesome songs with their steam machines. I lay on an old army cot I called my bed and wondered where they were headed and if Ed was on or in one of their boxcars. I sure hope he was inside somewhere because it was fierce, exposed. Ed had been gone a couple of months this time and he'd written Mama a letter or two that was full of strange names and things. When he did come home, he'd sit around listening to the flights of wild geese overhead . . . sitting silentlike, with a half-smile on his face as though he was packing his trunk in his mind, fixing to leave again.

Papa was roaring snoring, and I drifted off to sleep counting the times he snored before he'd change pitches.

Morning sounds woke me up to the clearest, coldest day we'd had up to now and I had to hit the road running 'cause I had me a job cutting pulpwood. I had to make me some money for Christmas and this was the only work I could find. Me and John were sawing on the same team and without gloves; the old crosscut saw was getting its pound of flesh. I had a big raw blister on my right hand and had wrapped a piece of muslin around my palm to give me a little ease. This weekend, I was going to Monroe and buy me a pair of gloves.

We stacked what we'd cut the day before and started in on our new swath. Tuesday morning and it was cold. It's bad enough to cut wood in summer but this was a long row with a dull hoe chore. When we knocked off for lunch, I sat down under a big old "hicker-nut" tree amid the signs of squirrels having dined before me. There had been many meals enjoyed on the limbs above, and below by forest creatures that never climbed a tree, including a herd of wild hogs, gleaning the harvest of nature.

I smelled of coal oil as I bit into my biscuit sandwich. My blister seemed unaware of the constant care I'd given it, but the kerosene did seem to soothe it some.

The days seemed all the same, saw and stack, saw and stack, and three more days were gone. I was toughening to the task and when we finished eating our meager meal, I got up, stretched, and picked up my Coke bottle filled with coal oil.

I stuffed the pine needles into a tight wad in the throat of the homemade sprinkler and coated both sides of the cross-cut to ease the draw of the rosin. I thought it funny that we used a product from the tree to speed the saw that fells the forest.

Waking up that Saturday was just like waking up on Monday 'cept I didn't dread the day. I was gonna catch me a ride to Monroe and do me something besides window-shopping and wishing.

When we'd sold our cords of pulpwood Friday evening, we got $6.83 apiece and felt richer'n Bim Gump on his Australian goat ranch.

I caught a ride with Earl Barron, got off in front of the Capitol Theatre, and was tempted to go see Buck Jones ride off into the sunset, but my need for gloves came first. I walked down by E. Jack Selig's and looked at the clothes, then went on to Ward's. I noticed the fellow who'd showed me the French-toed shoes, and when he saw me he busied himself. I guess he didn't want to sell any more eight-cent soles. . . . Well, he didn't know he was missing a cash sale. I picked through the gloves and settled on the split leather. They cost me thirty-nine cents, but they were worth it. I coulda bought some all-cotton ones for nine cents, but they weren't tough enough for sawing.

I started out of the store and almost made it when I saw it! Prettiest pocketbook I ever eyed. I asked the clerk if I could just look at it. The salesman said it was a brown calfskin with goat lacing around the edges, and it only cost $1.95. I coveted it and knew I was had. I didn't have any money to put in it, but I had my first grown-up wallet. I counted my money and was down to less than twenty cents. I'd already paid Papa the $4.32 I'd been owing him. So I was going to have a lot of pulpwood to cord next week, if I was going to tote any money in that pocketbook.

My Christmas holidays were just about over and I had nothing to buy presents with. Monday came quicker'n Friday and I walked up to the pine thicket with my saw, coal oil, sack of biscuits, and new gloves. The wood man was sitting in his pickup when I got there.

"Howdy," he hailed me, and without giving me a chance to howdy back said simply, "we're through heah; we draggin' up."

I got right in the middle of the Noel season with seventeen cents. I knew what Papa was gonna get for Christmas—a new pair of split-leather gloves, smelling slightly of coal oil. And I only owed $2.00 again for the present I got for Mama.

Friends who advise "it'll all come out in the wash" seldom point out that it all goes down the drain too!

SAVED BY A NOSE

One of our friends was having a birthday party and I was invited. The only trouble was, so was my brother. That meant one of us couldn't go 'cause we only had enough clothes for a one-person party. I, being the youngest, lost out.

The party was at night and that was much more fun, 'cause we were at the age where girls were girls, not just someone else at a party.

I had already resigned myself to my fate and then I struck upon a way I could go to the get-together and still be accepted. I would go hunting, for even though night hunting with a light was against the law, during the depression many things were winked at.

I put on rubber knee boots, an old ragged shirt and breeches, loaded my carbide light, put four or five shells in my pocket, and went to the cupboard to get some kitchen matches. I picked up my old double-barrel twelve-gauge and struck out.

I arrived at the party with two swamp rabbits hanging from my belt to the shrieks of the girls and smirks of the boys.

Beyond the familiar faces, I saw the bluest eyes and blondest hair I had ever seen and wished I was dressed good. I couldn't even talk; just every now and then I'd grin and point to my rabbits. I was so smitten by this girl from Monroe, I didn't even notice the smell of my old rubber boots. She was a city girl, so sure of herself.

It would be many weeks before she would see me again. I had been saving money outa every chore I could find, from selling coon hides to cleaning out chicken houses, but I finally scraped together $2.86. I caught a ride to Monroe and bought her a real pretty simulated mother-of-pearl manicure set with real make-believe red velvet. I caught a ride out close to her house and walked the other two miles.

A big dog met me with growls and warnings and accused me of smelling like country, but I woulda fought a lion to get to her. I eased past 'im saying, "Nice dog, good dog, nice dog," and knocked at her door. I was shaking so when she answered, I just kinda pushed the gift in her hands. Her eyes were as blue as I remembered and that blond hair was gleaming. There was a big, young fellow behind her and he walked up and put his arms around her shoulders. I faintly remember her saying, "This is my boyfriend, John Somebody," and "I can't remember your name." Then she said, "I can't keep this," but her knuckles were white as she gripped the gift and I knew she was going to.

What lot did fate have for me? Why? She didn't even remember my name. But I recall as she closed the door, for the first time in ninety days, I noticed she had a big nose!

I will always believe I heard her say, "Psst, git 'im," and the dog did.

I got over her by the time I got to the gate.

Illustrations and instructions are imperative when comprehension is the main shortage.

SHARING

Lloyd Swanson and I were buddies, and whatever he had, I had. Whatever I owned, he owned. If I had a dime, he had a nickel and if he had a dime, I owned five cents. It was share and share alike.

He courted a girl by the name of Lucille and I would go with him when he went to see her. Before we got to her house, we would flip whosever dime we had to see who would say, "I don't want a Coke." Cokes were a nickel apiece and somebody had to give. We could always depend on Lucille to say, "I'll take a Coke," 'cause she was perpetually thirsty and one of us better not be.

Lloyd and I had a deal worked out. Whoever won had to leave a big swallow in the bottle and whoever lost got to take the bottles back. So, the loser always got some Coke. But never from Lucille's bottle, because she could dry-clean 'em. It was so dry when she got through drinking, you could store powder in 'em.

But me and Lloyd learned to share.

Book sense is the logical way to conclude that common sense is an uncommon thing.

THREE LESSONS

I suppose we all learn something from someone as long as we live and I will be forever grateful to some of my teachers.

I don't just mean Mama and Papa or all the fine folks who tried and succeeded, to a degree, to inspire me through the years in school. Among those are "Tot" Godwin, Frances Guthrie, the Risers, Durhams, Hayes, Rushes, and Gilberts. I don't even mean the "learnings" we got from Sunday School or church; or the how-to-build character, faith, and confidence lessons from the likes of Addie Hoover or Jessie Royce; or the dignity of work lessons from Tom Davis, Claude Harrison, or Sam Walker.

I'm thinking of those who, through their daily living, imparted a piece of themselves and the things they did through common logic or a compelling force outside themselves that made us the brighter beneficiaries.

First

Old man Veaux was a ragpicker and as tattered as his trade. He eternally walked the roads and byways with a croaker sack over his shoulder, oscillating eyes sweeping the country for a picking. He never returned home without an inventory of bottles, cans, shoes, shirts, nuts, bolts, nails, or bits and pieces from each household's emissions. No ditch or creek bank escaped his gleanings. I have seen him walk along the middle of the Pelican Highway and spot a can or bottle, and without ever turning from his path aim the open end of that croaker sack toward his newfound treasure and—"scuzzaputt"—the object would disappear down the throat of that burlap bag, or so it is remembered through the eyes of that ten-year-old boy who thought he saw it.

I've often wondered why he gathered all the flotsam over these years. For after he died, most of it was found behind his house, neat and sorted, in rows and piles.

Over the decades that have come and gone, bringing more people, bottles, babies, cans, junk, or jewels, we who knew Veaux or watched and wondered at his actions were probably vexed or impressed, to some degree, by his strange harvestings and his prudence in culling nothing from his gatherings.

We, too, have paused to recover a bottle or a scrap of this or that and not even remembered it was a two-legged vacuum cleaner named Volley Veaux who taught us to pick up behind mankind so we would not be buried in our own debris.

Second

I asked the super for a job on the State Highway Department Project. They were blacktopping Louisiana 139, sometimes known as the old Monroe-Bastrop Highway. He threw back his head and laughed with scorn at the idea of a scrawny under-weight kid like me "toting" my load. I had never heard such vile language, and if he couldn't think of a "cussword," he'd just growl.

I stood and listened to his abuse until he finished. Then I made him this offer: "If I can't handle my shovel, not just for a day, but for a week, you won't owe me a dime. Whether I work four days or five, if I can't 'tote' my load, you can scratch my name from the time book and mark it free."

Then he said, "Look, ole Martin didn't make it, boy, and he could eat you for breakfast!"

I stood my ground and asked, "Deal or no deal?"

"Get you a shovel, boy."

He wasn't my teacher. My teacher came along late in the day in the form of a squat, fat Italian called Sam.

I was working like fury to prove my stamina, watching the "bay-windowed" super watching me.

The old Sam came walking by. "Hey, litta fella, coma wit me. Ima hear that fata man cussa you about a job. You justa watcha Sam."

Sam bent over and with the greatest of ease spread pea gravel across the roadbed as a baker would spread icing on a cake.

Without ever standing erect he had completed his job, bending to begin and straightening only when finished.

It dawned on me that it was the up and down, up and down, up and down that took its toll. So I was coupled with Sam from then on.

Sam could time our finishing to such a degree that if there was a shady spot twenty men down the road, we always happened to end up in the shade.

At the end of the first week, I proudly walked up to the timekeeper and drew my wages. The super was standing there watching and mumbling something under his breath.

I asked if he had said something to me.

He said, "Yeah, what you gonna do with all that money?"

I didn't say anything, but I thought I ought to give half of it to Sam.

When I told Sam how I felt, he just looked up and said with a wink, "You justa show somabody else, hey!"

So, I learned, don't watch the watchers . . . watch the workers.

Third

There were at least sixty of us, some old, some middle-aged, and a few like me still in high school. All of us were looking for a job. All but three of us were black.

Mr. Fite was the section foreman and was crippled on one side with a paralysis that caused him to limp and curl his hand into a fist. But he was tough, chewed tobacco, ran his crew like a general, and was a fair, honest man.

He walked out on his porch, spat his tobacco, wiped his mouth with the back of his hand, and said, "I don't need nobody." With that statement, he disappeared back inside.

We all turned and walked slowly down the lane away from the section house. I stopped and let the others walk past me. My friend, B.J., stopped and came back to where I stood. B.J. wanted to know what was wrong.

I pointed to the railroad and said simply, "As long as that railroad is, he's bound to need one more man, and I'm gonna go tell him so."

"That old man'll cut you up like his tobacco," snorted B.J.

"Well, he's gonna get a chance," I replied and walked back to his house.

I rapped on the porch floor and Mr. Fite came out and wanted to know if I hadn't been down there with the others.

I told him I had been and he wanted to know if I was "deef" or hard to understand.

I repeated my philosophy about the length of that railroad. Except I said it ought to be able to use two more men.

A slight smile showed briefly on his face and he asked, "What you mean, two men?"

I pointed down the lane to B.J. and said, "Him and me."

Mr. Fite asked, "How come he didn't come back with you?"

I said, "Well, sir, I guess he ain't as hungry as me."

He turned and walked back toward the door and said, "Hail him down here. Y'all take these applications to Dr. Hill in Monroe and I'll put you both to work."

I hailed B.J.

The next morning, I picked up a claw bar, an inanimate iron thing. It was used to dig under a spike in the railroad ties and extract the stubborn pieces of steel. I weighed about 130 pounds and the claw bar weighed 40. At the end of day, I weighed 120 pounds and so did the bar. I hung on tenaciously, all muscle and bone but just not enough of it. The second week, I grabbed that claw bar and wished that railroad track was not so long. Mr. Fite walked up the track toward me and called.

I headed back to where he stood and as I neared, he pulled out his old railroad watch. Without looking at me he said, "As of this . . ." and he waited for his watch to tick to a certain time, "moment, you are the water boy."

Little did I know, but I was to pick up that claw bar only one more time and gladly.

Each morning, I would put a block of ice in the wooden barrel and fill it with water. When we reached our designated area for work, a crew would unload the container and I would build a teepee of persimmon sprouts or anything else by the tracks. I kept a small square of canvas that I threw over the top of the barrel, and at quitting time I still had ice.

When the section gang called out, "Water boy," I would dip down into the cold clear liquid with my two galvanized buckets, hang my dippers on the bails, and run the rails. I quit walking the ties because too much water would be wasted by the sloshing.

The gang liked the way I gave service and I was on frequent call. The more water I delivered, the more water was wanted, until Mr. Fite called my hand.

"Water boy, you don't bring nobody no water no more until I call you 'cause nobody gets thirsty on this gang until I do."

"Yes, sir."

Mr. Fite was like a camel. He would wait until his crew was spitting cotton before he called. Of course nobody ever died.

One day, we finished our day's work and loaded up our tools and the water barrel. We always rode to and from our job on a motor car and a dolly car. The motor car was a four-wheeled rig with an air-cooled engine and the seats were in bench form, running from front to back on each side—no top, no windshield, just a way to ride. The dolly car was the same, except it had no motor.

I always folded my tarpaulin into a square and used it as a cushion on the bench. Mr. Fite was sitting up front as usual. I sat beside him. The motorman, with his back to Mr. Fite, sat on the driver's seat. A stick stuck up from the motor that, when pulled back, engaged the clutch. We were putt-putt-putting along when it began to rain. I rose up enough to slide my tarp from under me and wrapped it around my shoulders, staying relatively dry. All of us were lost in our thoughts, when a sudden gust of wind blew my makeshift rain gear off and the shock of the cold wind caused me to go, "WHEE OOOH!"

Everybody on the motor car and dolly flew from their perches like so many birds taking wing, except me and Mr. Fite. He didn't jump because he was lame. I didn't jump because I knew I wasn't a train whistle.

I grabbed the controls and kept the motor car rolling. Mr. Fite cussed us to Swartz. When we got to the section house, I braked the contraption, grabbed a claw bar, uncoupled the dolly car, and derailed the two. Mr. Fite was still fuming.

The next morning, the full crew arrived, loaded up, and left with no one making much about the flight.

Several years later, after I had married, joined the Marines, and fought in World War II, I returned home. Mr. Fite had since retired, moved to the city, and dreamed of a section of railroad in perfect condition.

I went by to see him and when I walked up to his door, I heard a familiar voice boom out, "Come on in, 'water boy.'" He was to call me this until he died.

I asked him why he had not fired me that day, for I knew he knew it was I. He sat for a moment and smiled. Then he said, "Well, 'water boy,' I never seen a section gang move so fast in my life and I never before saw a whole crew of men fly over a fence. It was a funny sight, but I just had to cuss a little bit."

I learned a lesson from that old gentleman. It takes more tolerance than water to run a railroad.

To try to bluff one's way through life is like renting a gun to get by a bear's nest—there's usually more than one bear.

MARY AND THE MOVE

When a poor family moves from a hovel to a hovel, it's just a move, but when you are affluent to a degree and move from a house to a hovel, it's really not a move, it's a trauma. And so it began during the depression. We ate well but we weren't in the ranks of the rich and many people during the hard years joined our category.

Mary's family was among the traumas. Her father moved the family to the old store building—no running water, no indoor bath, just a big old wooden building with a tin top.

The reason I had such compassion for this family was because their youngest child was a girl about my age and she had dark eyes, long flowing black hair, and an olive complexion. Besides, she was well figured and easy to talk to. I don't know if I would have had such empathy had Mary been ugly. I could not bear to think of her not having the conveniences she was accustomed to, so I determined I would be her benefactor.

I scrounged the countryside for pipe and materials and soon had water and gas hooked up for her bath. I had to find something to substitute for a hot-water heater and I used an old round gas tank from an early vintage Dodge. I placed it upon four firm legs and installed a burner underneath. There was no chance for it to explode, for the water was let into the tank with a faucet located over the spout that gasoline had been poured in, and the water was drawn off from the fuel line end.

I lit it up and soon the water was stirring and groaning. I was so proud of my ingenuity, I could hardly contain myself. It was not a tiled bath, but it beat bathing in a bucket.

I found a mound of dirt across the road from the old store and waited until she finished her bath. Soon Mary came through the front door, brushing her long hair until it gleamed. I shall never forget the sight of her. Red dress, dark flashing eyes, and at any moment I knew she would call to me. I felt not unlike a knight of old, waiting for a beckon from his lady. I stood up, ready for her signal, and then a Model A Ford drove up in front of the old store and without even a wave, she was gone.

I don't know why fate did that to me then, nor have I ever understood, but fate also deals other strange hands. For Kirby brought Mary home within a short time, because he was allergic to gasoline and Mary smelled like ethyl the first three times she used my homemade hot-water heater. She would glow whenever anyone lit a match near her for a month. Well, her folks got to doing better and moved back to Monroe. We got to doing better and moved into the old store.

But ours was just a move.

If I had been born with a silver spoon in my mouth, it'd be my luck my teeth woulda tarnished.

SHORTCHANGED AT CHRISTMAS

Mr. Guy had passed away a few days before the holidays and it fell to Mrs. Guy's lot to run the store. It was cold even on cool days with the old building's tin top, single floors, and thin walls, but that didn't bother Mrs. Guy because she pulled her part of the load more'n most. Nevertheless, Ma Taylor was called in to give moral support—what with Sarah datin', Lloyd huntin', and Mary spendin' the week with some of her friends from Monroe.

Well now, it just might have been known or it may not have, but the first day when everyone was gone, two would-be bandits came bustin' in with bandanas around their faces and collars upturned. Ma Taylor cackled out at the sight of 'em and cajoled both of 'em to quit playing desperados and take them fool rags off their faces. The bandits brandished their old revolvers and warned her to "shut yer howling face before we blow yer head off," but Ma Taylor just hollered the louder, slappin' her leg and sayin' things like "I know both you young whippersnappers and I oughta whup yer backsides and send you back to yer mamas!"

"Jes' shut up, you crazy ole woman," one of 'em shouted and turned his attention to Mrs. Guy behind the counter.

What the robbers didn't know was, there were two drawers built under the counter for the money. One was a long drawer for the folding money, the other a shorter one for the silver and copper coins.

"Gimme yer money, mam, and right now, 'fore I shoot you dead," growled one of the nervous robbers, tryin' to imitate a Saturday cowboy movie star.

"We don't have any money, young man" was Mrs. Guy's reply. She was shaking inside but was surprised at her calm. Then she continued, "Here, take this sack and get you some bread or food and leave us alone."

"We ain't leaving 'til we git yer money," he exclaimed, becoming more intimidated, 'specially with Ma Taylor's unceasing needling.

"Gimme that peashooter, boy. I'll show you how to rob a poor widder woman, and lemme borrow your bandana to dry my eyes. I'm laughing 'til I've cried!" Ma kept up her barrage.

"Shut up, I said." He gestured as if to strike her with the pistol.

Mrs. Guy, fearin' for Ma's safety, said, "Young man, there's the money drawer. Now take it and get out of here!" With that, she turned and walked toward the back of the old store. The young thief was unwittingly pointed to the short drawer and in his anxiety to get the loot and leave, he snatched at the handle. The short drawer came quickly out of its moorings and scattered coins asunder. It was such a shock to the two lawbreakers that they fled without a dime. Ma Taylor scurried after them with a broom, laughin' and sendin' 'em off with, "I told you dumb deadbeats to git!" and git they did!

The old gravel road boiled up after their A Model getaway auto as they vanished out of sight. Mrs. Guy swept the coins into a pile and sorted them back into their respective places in the drawer. Ma Taylor walked back inside and with a sigh said, "If that don't beat all. Stealing is bad enough, but trying to rob somebody a week before Christmas! It just beats all!"

"Yes," replied Mrs. Guy, "but this depression has a lot of folks doing things they wouldn't ordinarily do."

"I suppose so," said Ma. "Seems a shame though." The door of the old store opened and Lula came in with her big black face shining and smiling as usual. "Howdy, mam," she beamed.

"Hello, Lula, can I help you?"

"Yes'm, I needs me a piece of dry salt for my greens, jes' a tiny sliver."

Mrs. Guy cut off a nice chunk, wrapped it in thick paper, and without weighing it handed it to Lula saying, "We'll catch it next time, alright?"

"Oh, thank you, Mrs. Guy, much obliged, much obliged."

The next morning Lula would be out early, and Mrs. Guy would be paid for the salt meat when she brought in the bread, for it would be garnished with a family-sized bundle of greens, picked, washed, and ready for cookin'.

People shared back then for they cared back then, and I learned in those years that some people who had plenty and could have given really couldn't because of selfishness. Others who had little and couldn't afford to give, did give because of love. And so it is—those who can don't and those who can't do, and neither will ever understand the other. Some never learned the lesson taught many years ago by a young Hebrew from Bethlehem.

Collards are to greens what Adam is to man: the first in their species.

OUTTA SNUFF

Me and Papa had driven down to the depot at Swartz 'cause Mama had bought a hundred chickens from Ward's and they'd sent a card saying they were in.

Mr. Griffin was the agent, and when we got to the station there was a bunch of folks after their orders, too. We waited our turn and Papa talked to the mister for a while 'n then he walked out with a big square box with holes all 'round, so's the biddies could breathe.

Papa called to me to fetch another box that Mr. Griffin had for him, and I knew it was a "Top-Fill-Fount" to water the baby chicks with by the picture on the box's side. We crawled in our old car and headed home. Mama said you could order chicks cheaper'n you could raise 'em and I figgered she was right. 'Sides, an old setting hen was as persnickity as a grouchy man with the pips. Many a time I have slapped an old dominiquer for pecking me and all 'cause I had to make sure she wadn't claiming a fresh-laid yard egg. I've seen many an old hen that woulda been a good redheaded woodpecker, the way they could make a hole in your hide.

I was lost in the peep, peep, peep of our new crop of chickens when Papa braked our old car to a stop. I looked up and there was the ugliest old woman I'd ever seen, standin' in the middle of the road, swinging a possum back and forth like a flagman's lantern.

Papa hailed 'er and asked what was ailing her. She wailed like a snared rabbit. "I got this here possum fer sale fer five cents, 'cause'n I'm outta snuff."

Papa said, "We don't eat possum."

"Well," she said, "I ain't gonna move 'til you develop a taste fer it, 'cause I need a can o' snuff."

"I'll give you some Prince Albert for the animal," Papa countered.

"Where's it at?" she screamed.

He took his tin of tobacco out, scratched at the contents, and dumped a portion out into his palm. By then she was standing at the driver's door holding out her hand.

Papa gave her the alms and she dropped her possum, which forthwith quit grinnin' and took to the woods.

The old woman wadded the P.A. in a ball and wolfed at it. She placed the tobacco in her jaw and before Papa could git the old car rolling, she had puckered up and leaned back for a shot at the radiator cap. She woulda hit it, too, if it hadn't been a moving target.

Papa pulled the spark and gas levers down and shot out of range just as she was priming her pump for another shot. She turned on her heels and hit the woods running.

Mama was waiting on the porch when we got home. We busied ourselves and got the chicks in their coops and under the brooder light. We filled the feeders with Purina chick chow and separated the two or three puny ones to a box by the kitchen stove. I filled up two fruit-jar tops with water and a couple of more with feed and placed them in the makeshift hospital for the sick chicks. One of the little ones had a broken leg and I wrapped it up as best I could.

As I look back on those years, I recall the lame chick grew into a pullet, then a full-grown hen—never ever being in danger of being eaten because of her game leg. People just don't eat a fowl with a broken leg. She followed me around like a dog, and turned out to be one of our best laying hens, singing and hopping around on her one good leg. I called her "Crippled Little," and she lived out her life, finally dying of old age.

I learned at a very young age that to be lame, blind, or deaf does not necessarily mean one is handicapped.

Deterioration is a product of lack of determination.

101

MAKE IT A GOOD DAY

Sometimes we became very distraught, even though back then we didn't know what it meant, over our lot in life. We knew duck hunters had hip boots and waders because we had seen the pictures in the Ward's catalogue, but of course we couldn't order any.

We used tennis shoes and blue jeans and it was so cold wading the Boggy Boeuf that our legs became the color of our jeans, but once you were in the water it wasn't so bad. It was the "gittin'" in and "gittin'" out that would make you want to move three shirt sleeves south.

We would traverse the brake for half a day, out to Boiler Ridge and back, looking for greenheads. Ofttimes before noon we'd have ten or eleven, sometimes even more, but it was always the same good hunting if you could cut the cold. Mama could cook anything where it was better than it first sounded or looked and she didn't lose any ground on fixing wild game. One duck or a dozen, it was all the same to Mama, and it was always delicious.

After a hunt one winter's morn, we had climbed out of the swamp close to Hancock's Spur and built us a fire that would make Chicago's episode seem like a simmer. We stood around steaming as our clothes dried out. We picked the ducks as we thawed and soaked up enough heat to get back home with just the right amount of good memories to go back again.

As I think back, I am sure those naked ducks looked mighty indigent, but it helped with the preparation for the pot and Mama appreciated it. We would spend hours in the woods, just knocking around looking for signs of animals and bee trees to rob. The freedom of a country boy was endless and we used it. Some of the pleasures of that time are lost forever: the long, lonesome moan of an old freight train chugging along with its steam engine belching smoke, the all-day flight of ducks from some Northern clime, the well riders frozen to their saddles as they checked the meters, the old peckerwood sawmills, the whine of a Model T Ford turning a corner or the sound of an old Chrysler's gear singing when you'd shift into second, the smell of an old smokehouse.

It makes me proud that I lived in those times. All of us miss some things in our generation, and these are ours. From a flat-bed wagon to the age of rocketry—we ain't seen nothin' yet! Every day can be a good day and it's left up to us to make it so.

Men who curse the rain are the same who damn the dust.

MAMAS AND BOYS

Tadpoles and minnows scurried in frantic confusion as the foreign tan thing splashed noisily into their domain, then another and another until eight or nine naked bodies had hit the swimming hole—a hollering, howling, laughing mess of skin. Nobody ever drowned, but it's a wonder what with all the wild abandon and frolicking of the unbridled joys of boys.

My brother, Carl, climbed up an old snag of a tree to dive in, and when he came up he turned the muddy waters red. We all gathered around him to pull him to the bank, for he didn't even know he had a deep gash down his chest until we pointed it out to him. We never knew, nor did he, whether he had gotten his wound before or after he hit the water, but it broke up the party.

The whole wet wad of us ran down to Buckley's house and got Horace to daub him with coal oil. Of course we all held Carl down while it was going on and he bucked and bellowed, but old Horace doctored him like he was a hog. When we turned him loose we had to catch him again—but by then old Carl swore he was well, so we started looking for something to eat.

It just seemed fitting, since old Horace was so good to us and my brother, to raid his corncrib and turnip patch. Dry corn and raw turnips never tasted so good.

I guess if you wait long enough even blue John and tripe would be a covered-dish delight. We hadn't waited quite long enough, but we ate. When we got through eating, we all got our heads together to come up with some kind of lie to tell Mama. We'd already told most of those we'd heard, but Calvin Reeveas said we could say a black panther jumped us from the palmettos and everybody knew there'd been a big cat seen there since Old Red had tangled with him.

Mama was sitting on the porch when we got home and old Carl just rushed up and blurted out about this panther cat clawing him and how we hollered and whupped him off and how lucky we were to have saved him. Mama, who had sat on the judgment seat before, asked who poured coal oil on him.

"Mr. Horace did, himself," Carl said.

"I see," said Mama, very calmly, too calmly.

"Well, you jes' wouldn't a believed it, Mrs. Addison," one of the clan countered.

Mama then asked the damning question. "How did he claw you that bad without tearing your shirt?"

Mama won the case without rebuttal. Old Carl knew the cut on his chest was going to quit hurting as the pain became more acute on the lower part of his anatomy. I just got mine without anyplace to compare it to. Then Mama turned to seeing to it that the cut was cleaned and dressed properly, never once checking the two blistered bottoms of her boys.

Carl asked Mama how come she had caught on so fast to our lie. Mama just said quietly, "Look at your hands." What we saw were four still-wrinkled hands from the soaking in the creek.

Boys and mamas never change, and thus, boys will always be caught, whipped, cured, and loved—and mamas will always be heard saying, "If you go in that nasty creek and drown, I'm going to beat you to death!"

Which has only one answer: "Yes'm."

Some of the things we looked forward to with great dread, we now look back on with appreciation that we were part of it and we are proud to have been there.

SETBACKS TO SCIENCE

I was so weak from my annual siege of calomel, castor oil, and swamp fever that my frail body was mostly bones and very little matter. I was a sickly child, being killed by the "cure." Mama had hovered over me for years trying to get me on the road to health, and seemed to be on a cold trail. Then came the crash.

The depression was a cruel exposure, but in a strange way, my kindest friend. Mr. Guy moved his family out to the corner of Louisiana 139 and Thunder Road, and one of his children was a lanky drink of water named Lloyd.

One day, Lloyd and I were strolling along the lane toward my house. We were a contrast in physiques: one muscular, one emaciated. Without warning, he did a half-cartwheel and stood on one hand. He balanced himself, holding his left hand behind his back, thumb looped in his belt. Lloyd eased himself down into an upside-down chin-up, then just as suddenly, leaped back in an arc landing on his feet. I stood in awe at this fantastic young man. He walked on down the lane without waiting for me. I ran after and walked silently beside him.

Lloyd stopped and asked two questions: "How long you been sick?" and "Would you like to be able to do that?"

"I been sick ever since I caught that swamp fever," I answered. "And I ain't gonna never be able to do whatcher jes' did."

"We'll see," he replied and like an afterthought said, "I've got a barbell set."

Week after week, we worked together. I was too weak to lift more than the bar at first, but after much patience with me, Lloyd started adding the lighter weights until I could easily lift them. Then he would add more as I progressed. By the end of the summer, the change was evidenced in my shoulders, chest, and biceps; my whole body had been built into a healthy young man. I'd never felt so good! My energy was boundless and the next year I did not have chills and fever and was able to do most of the presses that Lloyd could do. There was never a dull moment around him.

I recall one day he confided in me about a secret experiment he wanted to try, and he needed an aide. He also wanted me to supply some very important experimentees for the project. He needed one bullfrog, several toads, a live bird, any kind, and one dead buzzard. I soon had his order filled and we met in our laboratory, which usually served as the feed house for our cows and hogs. I had scrubbed the shelf clean with "casin'head" gas and Lloyd put on a pair of rubber gloves and handed me a pair. We were very sterile in our project. Lloyd put on his mask and handed me mine. It was the first and last time I was to use a sanitary napkin, but they were great for our medicinal masks.

Then Lloyd said, "We need to remove the gastric juices from the buzzard's stomach and inject it into each specimen. We'll use the bullfrog first, then the toads. Let's save the jaybird 'til last."

It was a solemn scene as we worked in our coal-oil-lit laboratory, revolutionizing the world of medicine with our cure for cancer. Lloyd had concluded that if a buzzard could digest anything, this could surely do the same to the dreaded cells of malignancy. Neither I nor Lloyd would ever know if it would or could have worked. Our inoculatees were discovered by an old mama pig who did not know or give one whit about our arduous approach to a scientific breakthrough, and she devoured frog and all for breakfast. However, our thoughts had gone on a different tangent and did not bother us anymore than they had the sow.

Shortly after our endeavor in the field of research, the Guys moved to Monroe. I did not know where Lloyd lived after that time, except his place in my memories.

The weekend after Lloyd left I was to spend with C. G. Pearce, an old friend whose family had moved to Monroe. Perhaps I would see Lloyd in town. The next morning when I walked into the bathroom, I found C.G. blowing out a "kitchen match."

I stated, "I didn't know you smoked," in a half-question.

"I don't," he replied and explained. Those were the days before air freshener and he was relying on sulphur for the same. I was delighted over my newfound knowledge, and when I got back home I was determined to expose Papa to the revelation discovered at the mecca. It was a dismal failure. Not only did it not work, but more, I burned the fool thing down.

Papa was very philosophical about it all and said, "Well, we needed a new outhouse, anyway."

I discovered at a very early age that a little learning is a dangerous thing.

The growth of one's potential has been kept in bondage many times by insecure superiors.

HOGGING THE MARKET

Spring was dogging winter's coattail and we had already started breaking ground for this year's garden. I was counting up all my sales that I had made and delivered, because I had sold enough "Ferry Seeds" to win a genuine regulation-size guitar. I couldn't play one, but Papa could pick or puff on anything that made music and get a tune out of it. I followed my instructions to the letter on mailing in the monies and getting credit for my achievements. The next few weeks were going to be the hard ones, waiting for my prized instrument. Every day, when I got home from school, I would rush in to ask Mama if I had gotten any mail.

Then it happened. Sitting just inside the door was my reward. I ripped off the cardboard to expose the prettiest guitar I had ever seen, which wasn't much of a yardstick . . . but I thought it was and started right away to learn the chords.

Papa was sitting out on the porch reading the paper and called for me to fetch the thing out to him.

The first step he took was to tune the strings, and then he played a little ditty called "Never Loved but One Girl in My Life." Then he taught me how to play it. I still know how to play it and that has been over fifty years ago. Of course, that's the only tune I can play, even to this day. . . .

I would pick on that guitar 'til my fingers got so sore that I could hardly pick up lint. I never did sound like Tex Ritter or any other cowboy star but I did have the determination to keep trying. I know the folks were delighted the day Mr. Newt Walker came over to our house and offered to trade me a sow pig that was springing for my guitar. My aching-eared parents encouraged me to take the deal. So I started on a new career of raising hogs.

I fed that black beast everything that she would eat. She would eat anything and everything made her fat. The day grew nearer to the time her litter would arrive and I became more excited with each passing hour, counting my pigs before their debut.

One day I got off the old school bus and headed for the hogpen. When I arrived, the fence was torn open and Mama hog was gone.

I ran back to the house, changed into some old clothes, and headed for the woods. I looked in the gullies, briar patches, treetops—everywhere I thought the old sow would build her nest to bear her brood. Nothing, I found not a trace of her or her family. Each day when I got home from school and then on the weekends I searched, but in vain.

Then, after about two weeks, I gave up the charge and decided she was gone. Over the years, I have wondered about my short tenure in the pork business. Even now, I have been unable to put the happening out of my mind. For I keep thinking that had she had a litter of six and they had had a litter of six and then they each had litters of six for the past fifty years, and if I could find her and my other "claim" in the woods—approximately 8 million, more or less—I'd be literally rich and surely have more sausage than Jimmy Dean has at hog-killing time.

A hog doesn't mind living in garbage, but of course he began his life in a litter.

If we never made mistakes no one could afford us. Thus, through these imperfections we are employable and since we all cannot do like chores with the same dexterity, we must depend on others to help in our different endeavors. Knowing these truths, we should exalt each other's talents instead of rushing in to condemn at the first sign of faltering. For if we must work together, let us work together.

Harry Wayne Addison

Oh God, before I lapse into the twilight of senility, grant me the sanity to lay aside my illusions of grandeur that I may pass the yoke of decision on to the astute minds of the young.

THE PAUSE